God's Garden Tools

Tools From The Bible
To Develop A Deeper Walk With God

Gina R. Burns

God's Garden Tools

CONTENTS

PRAYING WIVES AND MOTHERS

Who will heed the call and become a
steadfast Praying Wife and Mother?

Who will fall to her knees on behalf of
her family knowing that the Lord for her
will intercede?

Who will be willing to cry out and shed tears
for those who are dear to her heart?

Who in the middle of the night will lay her hand
upon the ones she loves so dear and believe
her prayers are being heard?

Who will be willing to not grow weary
when her prayers seem to go unnoticed?

Who will persevere knowing that God Almighty
sees and recognizes the power of a
Praying Wife and Mother?

Who will give herself daily to lift her
family up to God? To cry out with her
heart for God's mercy and grace?

Will you be the one who will take a stand and
become a Praying Wife and Mother?

Will you rise and answer the call and
then bow upon your knees?

Will you freely give of your time
to lift up your family's needs?

Will you rise and answer the call
and be your family's voice?

Oh, the Power of a Praying Wife and Mother!

Foreword

What if you came to the dinner table and everyone but you had a nice, big, thick steak grilled to perfection with all the trimmings? The choicest of meat that was available was on their plates? Then at your plate you noticed you also had a steak with all the trimmings, except yours was in baby food jars, all pureed up. How would you react? What if someone looked at you and said, "We're all eating the same thing, it's just that yours is a little easier to digest?" You would probably throw those jars of baby food away and go and get yourself a real steak.

Just as babies cannot eat a "real" steak, we don't want to eat baby food. Yes, it's all nourishing and has vitamins but our bodies, as we get older, require the proper food at the proper time for development. Does it mean that babies food isn't needed, necessary or nourishing? Absolutely not! It's just their bodies can only handle that type of prepared food for where they are developmentally. We, as adults, have grown out of that stage and when we want "meat" we want real "meat" because our bodies need, require and can handle it.

We all from birth go from stage to stage in growing. As we grow and mature we can handle more in our lives because we become more and more responsible. It's a great and wonderful thing to be learning and growing all the time and experiencing new things. This Praying Wives and Mothers book is yet another stage for you to grow from. If you are seeking or a new believer we suggest you start with the companion book, God's Garden. Our Lord is so gracious in not "blasting" us face to face with His knowledge. He takes us right where we are and feeds us according to what we can handle. Now He's saying, "You've grown and matured and now I want to give you some 'meat.'" These lessons are longer and more in depth than the stories in God's Garden. He has taken you from the beginning stage and now that you've grown, He wants to give you even more of Him. It's very exciting and wonderful to be at a new stage of learning and growing with God, and you will love each lesson.

May God reveal Himself to you even greater than before. May He show Himself bigger and bigger to you every day. May you rest in

His love for you and may He fill you with His wisdom, understanding, knowledge, and revelation.

You have been invited to dine with The Lord your God for a steak dinner with all the trimmings. May you always be full. Full of Him and His riches.

God Bless You

Come and Walk With Me

Roller coasters are an amazing thing to look at. The way they are designed and programmed to run is fascinating. The speed, twists, turns are really are exciting and to see people's faces on them is also quite interesting. Some have a look of terror, and some have the look of terror and of fun, and most of them, for the most part, are enjoying the "thrill ride." Life also, at times, can be like that of a roller coaster ride because of all the ups, downs and twists, and can really try and test our faith, even for those who rely on God.

In Matthew 14:23-24 we read about Jesus and His disciples. In this passage Jesus tells the disciples to get into a boat and go to the other side of the lake while He dismisses the crowd that He was ministering to. As the disciples headed off to do this Jesus Himself went to pray alone for a while which ended up being until evening time. When He was done praying He saw that the disciples were out far from shore and He decided to walk on the water towards them. As Jesus was making His way to the disciples in the boat a great wind started to blow out on the sea. Verses 26-31 states, "the disciples then saw a figure coming towards them and cried out in fear saying, "It's a ghost." Jesus though immediately responded to them by saying, "Take courage! It is I. don't be afraid." Peter then says to Jesus "Lord if it is you tell me to come to you on the water." Jesus then gives Peter the ok and says "Come." Peter then gets out of the boat, and walks on the water towards Jesus, but as he was doing so he noticed the wind picking up around him. Peter then became very afraid and began to sink and cried out "Lord save me!" Immediately Jesus reached out His hand towards him and said "You of little faith" "Why did you doubt?"

This is a great story and yet the question is, what if Jesus had asked you to "walk out." What would you have done? Would you have been distracted and afraid of the wind that was starting to blow your way? Would you have made it all the way to Jesus or would the fear of what was happening around you cause you to sink?

I myself cannot imagine what that moment had to have been like not only for Peter, but also for the other disciples who were watching all this take place. Imagine what that moment had to have been like when Peter realized he was doing it. That he was walking on water. Then unfortunately, Peter's focus was shifted from that of Jesus and then on his circumstances.

The reality for all of us is that we live in a world that will always have twists, turns, and ups and downs, but we cannot allow ourselves to be focused on them. We have to continually keep our eyes, our focus on the Lord. For when we are fixed and focused upon Him, that's when the impossible is made possible. That is when we can do all things through Christ who strengthens us, as Philippians 4:13 states.

We have to also remember that the Lord we serve is bigger than any "wind" that blows our way. That we need to get to the place in our lives where are so rooted and grounded in Him that "worldly" circumstances do not affect the direction in which we are going. When that happens that is when although we may not be physically walking on water, but we will be doing some amazing things because of Jesus Christ. Even for Peter one needs to remember that he was the only one who got out of the boat that night so for that one needs to admire him even though he didn't make it all the way there and back- he did choose to get out of the boat!!

Are you willing to get out of your so-called boat and walk with Jesus? Are you willing to walk in the direction of Jesus despite what twists, turns come along to try and distract you? Are you willing to walk by faith and not by sight? If you are then that's when you are able to "walk on water" with your master and that is when the impossible is made possible.

Holes or Holiness

Suppose you had only one pair of socks to wear every day, and they were extremely "worn." Let's say the heal of those socks were wearing thin and were full of holes. Then suppose someone noticed your "holy, worn" socks and offered you a brand new pair, a real thick pair of socks. A pair of socks that were cushy feeling and kept your feet warm and well protected. What would you do? Would you keep the old ones because they were "worn-in" and somehow comfortable to you or would you gladly take the new pair?

This may sound like a strange question but in reality this illustration fits our lives. The "worn" socks are in effect our lives. Lives that have been shattered, hurt, and damaged. Lives that have major holes in them because of events in our lives. Things we will not let go of. Things like hurt, anger, resentment, and unforgiveness. Perhaps others caused the holes. Holes that were not created by you but you won't let go of them. Are you determined to hang on to them, so much so that you cannot let go of the old and reach for the new? The new socks represent forgiveness, kindness, gentleness, peace, joy, trust, and love and yet in order to receive these you have to let go of the old.

Ephesians 4:31 tells us, "Let all bitterness and wrath and anger be put away from you along with all malice. And be kind to one another, tender hearted, forgiving each other just as God in Christ also has forgiven you."

Sometimes we get so "comfortable" that we don't know how to change or to even accept change. We decide that we'll make the change when the other person that hurt us makes the first move. That person, one needs to realize, may never attempt to make the move you're expecting, but you can. Unforgiveness for one causes "holes" in our lives. Pretty soon the "hole" will get so large that the bottom falls out. The weights of bitterness and anger build on top of unforgiveness and it gets out of control.

You cannot go back and undo all the hurts and wrongs done to you but you can choose to move forward. You can choose to do away with "holy worn out socks" and choose to be clothed in Christ and always be warm, perfect, and always protected and loved. If you have "holes" or "worn out" places in your heart let go of all of it and let Him cover you in His love and peace. Decide what you really need and desire. Is it "Holes" or "Holiness"?

Life And Death In Our Tongue

How many times have we said, "I don't know how were going to make it" or "I guess we are always going to struggle?"

Perhaps we have even said, 'There's no cure for this disease, the doctors say there's nothing they can do." Statements like these reflect "death" because there is nothing positive in these or in similar statements. Nothing alive or bringing forth hope. A better way to say things would be, "things are tight this week, but God will provide." Also, in the statement, "there's no cure for this disease and the doctors say there's nothing they can do", could be replaced by, "by His stripes we are healed."

According to Proverbs 18:21 which says, "Death and life are in the power of the tongue" so we need to watch the words which come out of mouths. So instead of "Things will never work out" how about "With man this is impossible, but with God all things are possible" which is what Matthew 19:26 tells us. Or that according to Matthew 6:30 we don't have to worry about not having enough because "God will clothe and feed us."

We have the power each day to choose what we're going to say and what we are going to believe. Either we believe God's word and receive it for our lives or we don't and based on that we must make a choice to not go on what we see and feel. The Bible warns us not to be "double - minded" which means saying, "Ok Lord, you take this situation and handle it," and then we take it back and worry and speak "death" words concerning it. What needs to come out of our mouths instead should be words of life for why would we want to say out loud what Satan's plan for us is? He only wants us in poverty, full of sickness and not to have any hope. He wants us to believe that so why give him the satisfaction when we have the hope of the Lord living inside of us? The words that come out of our mouths daily should only be God's word despite the situation we're facing, or what we're feeling at the time, and not live by what we see even if it is negative. 11 Corinthians 5:7 tells us, "For we walk by faith, not by sight." So, for us, let's purpose to not go by what we see, think, or feel, but only by what God's promises are for, and that is life!!

Walking Through

How many times do we find ourselves in situations that seem "hopeless"? Situations that look as though they are never going to get any better? When those happen to come into our lives it can be easy to think, "am I going to get through this?" or "when is this going to end? Where is the light at the end of the tunnel?"

Psalms 23:4 tells us, "Even though I walk through the valley of the shadow of death, I will fear no evil, for you are with me; your rod and your staff comfort me."

Many of us are familiar with this passage, but let's break it down a little further. The word "through" means, "Into one side, end or point and out the other." The word "valley" means, "Level or low land between mountains, hills or highlands." The word "staff" means, "A shaft or pole that forms a support or handle."

So, based on a few key words, we can find great comfort and assurance that God is not going to allow us to stay in that hard situation forever. That while for a time it may be difficult, we are to find comfort in even of the words through and staff. We have to believe that based on these words, we are going to come out of our "situation", and also that God is going to be the support and comfort that we need even at what seems to be the lowest point. Also the words, "Fear Not" need to bring comfort to us in that although it's simple we do not need to fear because He above all is with us and making a way out.

Isaiah 41:10 reminds us of this, "Do not fear, for I am with you, do not anxiously look about you, for I am your God. I will strengthen you. I will help you, surely I will uphold you with my righteous right hand."

The word surely means, "certainly" and certainly means, "without a doubt." The last three things to take from this are that we have His rod and His staff and they comfort us. The word "staff" means, "A shaft or pole that forms a support or handle." The word "comfort" means, "A state of mental or physical ease. Relief from sorrow or distress."

So now, since these words are broken down, we can be assured we will come out of our "mess" with God's help, protection, and comfort. We can know we are going to "walk through." We can walk through in peace and comfort because He is with us, holding onto us and comforting us. Know there is "light at the end of the tunnel." The light always has been Him and always will be!

Walking In Obedience And Blessing

Genesis 2: 15-17 reads, "The Lord God took the man and put him in the Garden of Eden to work it, and take care of it. And the Lord God commanded the man "You are free to eat from any tree in the garden; but you must not eat from the knowledge of good and evil for when you eat of it you will surely die."

Now to chapter 3:1-6, "Now the serpent was more crafty than any beast of the field which the lord had made. And he said to the woman, indeed, has God said, you shall not eat from any tree of the garden'? And the woman said to the serpent, from the fruit of the trees of the garden we may eat; but from the fruit of the tree which is in the middle of the garden, God has said, you shall not eat from it or touch it, least you die. And the serpent said to the woman, You shall surely not die! For God knows that in the day you eat from it your eyes will be opened, and you will be like God, knowing good and evil. When the woman saw that the tree was good for food, and that it was a delight to the eyes, and that the tree was desirable to make one wise, she took from its fruit and ate; and she gave also to her husband."

I can't imagine having God right in front of me commanding me not to do something and then choosing to do it anyways, and yet the truth is, we though do this exact thing every day. He may not be face to face with us as he was with them, but we know what He's telling us to do and not to do and a lot of times we willfully do the opposite. The word "crafty" in the dictionary means "Skillful in deceiving; cunning," and "cunning" means "Skill in deception." These words are the words describing to us who Satan is and his character, and that is why we need to avoid him. Because of Adam and Eve's disobedience, the Lord put a curse on them and he drove them out of the Garden in verse 23-24.

So many things in our lives that are "messed" up are because of our disobedience. We either flat out refuse to obey God or we let disobedience in and blame it on others. Just like forgiveness, maybe we refuse to forgive because it was "so and so's fault." We think we are not going to forgive until they apologize. So we then live in bitterness and disobedience.

Maybe it's with our children, we let things "slide" because others are doing it etc., when we know we are to discipline them and teach them the word of God, and to be an example to them of biblical principles.

We can get so wrapped up in, "Well I'm a good person, mother, wife, etc.," and we stop there. We don't really live in total obedience. Just like Adam and Eve, their disobedience did not just affect them, it affected everything from then on. They had everything they could have ever wanted, needed, and one choice changed the course of their lives, and ours as well.

When we live in obedience, even when its uncomfortable or everyone thinks we're crazy, we then receive the blessings from the Lord. It's not always going to be easy but we have to choose obedience above anything, which is truly an act of worship unto God. In Deuteronomy 28:1-14 the Bible lists what all the blessings are, and in chapter 30:1-10 we are reminded of what our rightful blessings are from God.

We all will have trials in our lives from time to time, but as God's children when were obedient we are under His protection of blessings. For the most part obedience is easy, but there are times when we're making a decision to do something, we need to think, "Does this line up with the Word?" If it doesn't, then we need to listen to God. We need to not worry about everyone else's opinion on what we should do because Gods opinion is the most important. Lastly, we need to be in Gods word daily. Spending time in prayer and finding out what He is saying to us and how we are to handle things. To be able to know God, and His ways, so we can walk with Him in total obedience and blessing.

God's Timing Or Mine?

One trait about myself that I wish I didn't have is my impatience to wait on things. At Christmas or on my birthday it drives me nuts to know there is a present somewhere in the house for me, and either I can't find it or if I do, it's already wrapped! There have been times when I have searched and found gifts my husband has gotten me, and I just couldn't stand it and I peeked!!! Now I know by me doing that I ruined the surprise for me, and then I ruined it for my husband. Even though he didn't know I peeked, my reaction was not what it should have been for him. I couldn't just be satisfied knowing there gift was promised to me. I took into my own hands and control and did what I wanted because I couldn't wait and because of that I ruined it.

There are times also when the Lord tells us something and because were tired of waiting, we take it into our own hands. The story of Abraham and his wife is a story similar to this very illustration. The Lord told Abraham in Genesis 15:4, "And, Behold the word of the Lord came unto him, saying, This shall not be thine heir; but he that shall come forth out of thine own bowels shall be thine heir. And he brought him forth abroad, and said, Look now toward heaven, and tell the stars, if thou be able to number them: and he said unto him, So shall thy seed be."

The Lord was telling Abraham in this passage that He was going to bless him with a son and that his descendants would be more than the number of the stars in the sky. Now the Bible does not specifically say that Abraham's wife Sarah would be giving birth to a child although given the fact that they were married it would make sense that the Lord was meaning the two of them together would bear children. One also needs to remember that this was not the first conversation God and Abraham had. Back in Genesis 12, God told him to leave his country when he was 75 years old and he did, so he must have believed and trusted in God or else he would not have left. There are a few more conversations up to this point that he and the Lord had together, and one could say that he trusted in the Lord and obviously knew Gods voice.

Look now in Genesis 16:1-6. The word of God tells us that Sarah felt that the Lord had prevented her from having children so she decided to take it in her own hands. She went to Abraham and said these words "Now behold, the Lord has prevented me from bearing children. Please go into my maid; perhaps I shall obtain children through her." And Abraham listened to the voice of Sarah. In Genesis 16:3-4 we also read, "And after Abraham had lived ten years in the land of Canaan, Abraham's wife Sarah took Hagar the Egyptian, her maid and gave her to her husband Abraham as his wife. And he went in to Hagar and she conceived, and when she saw that she had conceived her mistress was despised in her sight." The Lord then tells Abraham in chapters 17 that he and Sarah are going to have a child together and Abraham can't believe this. He says he's too old at a 100 years and Sarah at 90 years. Abraham tells his wife this and she just starts laughing. She doesn't believe it for a minute. God then asks Abraham, "Why did she laugh – is there anything too difficult for the Lord?" Well the story ends with Sarah conceiving and giving birth to their son who they named Isaac. Imagine for Sarah having to wait that long in life to have a child, and at that age. The Lord was faithful to His promise to Abraham in the end. If Abraham would have, though, just trusted that God was going to give him a child, through his marriage to Sarah, and waited, a lot of hurt could have been avoided. Think of the pain that was caused by this decision. I don't know any woman who would willingly let her husband do this sort of thing. Think of the jealously and bitterness it would cause, and did cause for Sarah and Hagar. Sarah desperately wanted children, as I'm sure Abraham did. To them this seemed like the only possible way and they chose it. They chose it out of desperation, and that choice caused a lot of pain for a lot of people.

There are several things to learn from this story:

1. Trust in the Lord 100% all the time. It doesn't matter what things appear to be. Trust what He has said to you.

2. Do not take things into your own hands because you are tired of waiting for the promise to come to pass. There is always a repercussion to others and to us when we do this. Seek His ways not your own ways.

3. Be in constant communication with the Lord. Listen when He speaks to you because you need His instruction, and obey whatever He tells you.

4. The Lord is faithful, 100% of the time. When He tells you something, it will come to pass. You may not know when or how but it will happen.

Abraham had to wait 25 years for Isaac, but the Lord also blessed him with 75 additional years with his son, because he lived to be 175 years old.

Now maybe you're thinking, "Well that's great for Abraham, because he had heard the Lords promise. What has God told me?" God's word to us has an answer for every question or problem we could ever have. If it's about marriages, finances, children, friendships, there is a word in the Bible for you.

So, He does have a word, a promise for every situation that we face. There is nothing that God does not have an answer for you about. Whatever you are believing God for trust me He will bring it to pass. Do not get discouraged when the manifestation of the answer isn't coming as fast as you want it to. He knows the perfect timing for every situation and He won't let you down. Sometimes we can tire of waiting and we take it into our own hands and then we end up regretting it later. We'll look back and say to ourselves, "I wish I would have just trusted and believed in God instead of taking it in my own hands, what a mess I'm in now." When the Lord tells us something we need to be patient and give it all to Him. To trust Him no matter how things look, and absolutely believe Him. He is on our side and His intention is not tease us, it's to teach us. Sometimes the "end-result" doesn't come when we want it too, but God Himself hasn't left us. He's still there teaching us things. Maybe the answer hasn't come to full manifestation because there are things we need to learn first. We are to always seek and believe God no matter how long it takes. To always remember that He knows better than us what is best for us, and when we need it. He doesn't need our "hands" in there messing with His divine plans. After all, He is God and we're not.

One Stone Away

When I became pregnant with our first child it required a lot of faith because the doctors said that if I continued with the pregnancy there was a chance it could cause major health problems, and possibly my life. I remember thinking though, I had God on my side despite what the doctors were saying. For the next nine months, I put all my trust and faith in God, that He would see me and the baby through, and He did.

The story of David and Goliath is also a story that required a lot of trust in God as well. It is a familiar story, but sometimes overlooked and can be found in 1 Samuel 17. The story is there was a boy named David who was the youngest of eight sons born to a man whose name was Jesse. Jesse sent David one day to bring food to his brothers who were involved in a battle between the Philistines and Israel. When David was there, he saw a giant named Goliath and asked some men nearby what the reward was for whoever killed him. The answer to this question was King Saul would give His daughter to the man who would kill Goliath and make this person's fathers house free in Israel. David brothers who were also standing nearby, were extremely irritated at David and asked him why he wasn't off doing his job of tending the sheep.

Shortly after this, King Saul heard about David inquiring about this giant and sent for him. David began to tell Saul that he would go, and fight Goliath and his God would keep him safe. Saul couldn't believe what he was hearing from this young man. David then goes on to inform the king that he has already killed a lion and a bear himself and said, "The Lord who delivered me from the paw of the lion and from the paw of the bear. He will deliver me from the hand of this Philistine."

Saul then proceeded to clothe David in his own personal armor as to help prepare him for the battle. David though took one look at it on him, and decided to not wear any of it, because it did not fit him. Instead he picked up five smooth stones from the brook, placed them in his shepherd's bag and proceeded towards Goliath. At this time Goliath was shouting at David, stating he was going to kill him. David however instead of running the other way shouts the same things back to Goliath but not quite exactly. David told Goliath that not only was he going to kill him, but that after he killed him, he was going to be-head him, and would do with it with the help his God.

Goliath didn't like these words shouted to him and started coming at David and David came towards Goliath. David then reached into his shepherd's bag, pulled out one stone, inserted into his sling shot and fired it at Goliath. The stone hit Goliath right between the eyes and actually sunk into his forehead killing him instantly. David then went and be-headed the giant like he said he would, and then it was over, just like that.

What an incredible story of courage, strength, determination and guts. Picture David being a teenager and going into battle with this giant and not really having anyone think he could do it. He didn't have his family on his side or any friends encouraging him. It was just him and his God, which in the end proved to be all he needed. Also, one needs to not forget that David didn't use the typical resources available to him for the battle, instead he chose something illogical. Something as small and seemingly insignificant as a stone. David also that day took a stand in front of everyone, and never flinched or backed away trusting in the Lord for his protection and to prevail and he did. David could have seen that giant as a threat, but he also deep down knew his God was bigger and more powerful that some giant that would come his way and that God would have the last say. Isaiah 54:17 reminds us of this very principle, "That no weapon formed against me shall prosper."

We all are going to face giants in our lives, but what matters is how we handle them. Will we run the other way, or will we run towards them in the name of our Lord? Are we going to choose to go into the battle knowing who we are in Christ? Are we going to trust God and give Him all the glory? Mark 9:23 says to us, "If thou canst believe, all things are possible to him that believeth."

You see David had the mindset that his God would deliver him and he already had the victory, so to him the threat of the battle was not really a threat because of who it was that he served! What an example his story is to us, for the things we face today that seem in our minds to be "giants." Each of us needs to remember the God David served and loved is the same God that is there for us. Whatever battle we may be facing is no "battle" at all to the Lord. He is just is looking for those who will stand up in the presence of their enemy and shout, "God is on my side and together we will have victory." So, the next time you happen to see a small stone lying on the ground pick it up and really look at it. Hold that stone in your hand and remember that for David it only took one. As you look at that stone remind yourself, that you yourself are only "one stone away" from victory. You have to believe it, claim it and receive it. Go into battle with the faith that God is on your side, regardless of what the situation looks like. Remember above all that He is your father and your strength and with Him all battles are always won!!

Walk By Faith And Not By Sight

In high school I tried out for the basketball team without any experience. I made the team, but not the varsity liked I had hoped, but the j.v. team. What else did I really expect! So, after that year of playing, learning, and getting some experience I felt like the next year I could make the varsity team if I practiced continually. So the following summer I asked our neighbors who had a basketball hoop in their driveway if I could practice shooting every day. They agreed, and I practiced every day. I would try all the shots I had seen done, and just kept at it continually every day. I knew I wanted to make the team, and either I gave up and quit, or I pressed in and stayed focused on my goal. The following season came, and I did make the varsity team in my junior and senior year. I lettered in basketball, and received a scholarship to a local college for a year. I'm not telling you this story to brag, but to tell you that we can't give up. Believe me when I say that first year, I played I was not very good, I'm not even sure why I even made the team. With discipline and a lot of prayer though I improved.

Sometimes we get discouraged when we think things are not happening as we want or as fast as we desire them to. We at those times just want to "give up."

In Luke 5:1-9 we read a story about a man named Simon who was a fisherman. Jesus was in Simons boat one day ministering. After Jesus was finished teaching He told Simon to "Put out into the deep water and let down your nets for a catch." Simon answered and replied back to Jesus "Master, we worked hard all night and caught nothing, but at your bidding I will let down the nets."

At this point Simon maybe is thinking, "I'm a professional fisherman, and we haven't caught anything all night. I'm tired, exhausted and now you want me to go fishing again, this is crazy." He was honest in what he said to Jesus, but yet he did obey even when it sounded crazy and illogical. When he did cast down his nets, there was so many fish that their nets began to break. They had to signal for help to their partners in another boat, because their boat was starting to sink from all the fish. Talk about a good harvest!

A lot of times in life we think, "That's it, I'm done." "I can't do this anymore, nothing is ever going to change." At those moments we need to really press in and believe God is making a way. That is what you call faith.

Hebrews 11:1 says to us this, "Now faith is the being sure of what we hope for and certain of what we do not see."

Hebrews 11:6 say this also to us, "Without faith it is impossible to please God, because anyone who comes to Him must believe that He exists and He rewards those who earnestly seek Him."

Sometimes we pray and pray for something, and we end up feeling like our prayers are not being answered much less being heard. I assure you that God hears and answers every request we make.

Psalms 91:15 assures also of this, "He shall call upon me and I will answer him. I will be with him in trouble; I will deliver him and honor him."

Isaiah 41:17 tells us, "When the poor and needy seek water and there is none, and their tongue faileth for thirst, I the God of Israel will not forsake them."

Galatians 6:9 say also, "Let us not become weary in doing good, for at the proper time (God's Time) we will reap a harvest if we do not give up."

Remember God hears our every request and knows our every need. He is always with us and most important He is for us. God promises our "Walking by faith and not by sight" and "Doing good" will be rewarded and not over-looked. Really what other choice do we have? We know and have the promise that He will reward us so why would we ever give up?

The Pit Was Meant For Good

The story of Joseph begins in Genesis 37 and goes into chapter 50. The story is about his family, hardships, forgiveness, and about family restoration.

Joseph's story in a quick version goes as follows. Joseph was the son of Jacob and he was his father's favorite son because he was born unto his father when he was late in his age. His father made Joseph a special coat to wear and his brothers became very jealous of him. Joseph also had two dreams and interpreted them. The dreams meant that his family would bow down to him one day and that made his brothers extremely angry. They decided to kill him, but Joseph's brother Reuben didn't want to do that, so he suggested they put him in a pit. His plan was to come back and rescue him, but the other brothers sold him to some merchants before Reuben could come back. They then took his coat and put goat's blood on it and took it to their father and said that an animal had attacked him and killed him.

Joseph was then taken to Egypt and lived with a man named Potiphar. Potiphar was one of Pharaoh's officials and he was well taken care of. Potiphar's wife though wanted Joseph to sleep with her and when he refused he left in a hurry and ended up leaving his coat there. She then claimed he tried to rape her, and from that accusation he was put in prison. The Lord though was with him in prison so much so that he was put in charge of all the prisoners. Two prisoners in that jail were the cupbearer to the king and the baker to the king. They both had dreams and had Joseph interpret them. The cupbearers dream interpreted meant that he would be released. The bakers dream was interpreted that he would be hung. When Joseph told the cupbearer his dream he asked him to remember him when he got out because he didn't deserve to be there.

It took two years for Joseph to be let out of prison. He was asked to interpret Pharaohs dream. When Joseph did this Pharaoh then let Joseph out of prison. Pharaoh then put Joseph in charge of the land of Egypt because of the famine that was going to come, which was his dream interpreted. Joseph's brothers ended up coming to Joseph not knowing who he was to buy grain for the famine at the request of their father Jacob. When they came, Joseph knew who they were but they didn't know who he was. (At this point Joseph's dream was fulfilled. They were bowing down to him because he was the Governor of the Land). In Chapter 45:5 we read how Joseph reveals himself to his brothers. Then he says to his brothers, "And now, do not be grieved or angry with yourselves, because you sold me here; for God sent me before you to preserve life." Eventually Joseph's father was told Joseph was alive and they were all restored to each other.

Jacob then dies 17 years later. He was separated from his son for at least 13 years but received an additional 17 years with him before he died. When Jacob died Joseph's brothers were worried that "What if Joseph should bear a grudge against us and pay us back in full for all the wrong which we did to him?" So they sent a message to Joseph saying "Your father charged before he died, saying "Thus you shall say to Joseph, "Please forgive, I beg of you, the transgression of your brothers and their sin, for they did you wrong." And now please forgive the transgression of the servants of the God of your father." It really doesn't say for sure if their father told them this or not, but Joseph had already forgiven them, even before he felt his brothers wanted forgiveness. Joseph tells them in verse 20, "And as for you, you meant evil against me, but God meant it for good in order to bring about this present result, to preserve many people alive. So therefore do not be afraid; I will provide for you and your little ones." We see that God clearly intended this for good. There's a lot to learn from this story, a lot of lessons. A few that are important are:

1. Jealousy always leads to destruction.

2. Even when we are in a "pit" God is always with us. He never leaves us, ever.

3. Everything is in Gods timing, not ours.

4. Forgiveness needs to come first even if the other person hasn't asked for it. Joseph not only forgave, but he also provided for them.

5. Family restoration is God's business no matter how hopeless things seem.

6. Looking at all situations, good and bad, and giving God all the glory. He's is control.

7. God also blessed Joseph's brothers and their families.

We all have experienced at least once of being in the "pit" like Joseph. Whether we were put there by others or by ourselves, we all have been there.

Psalms 40:1-3 reads as follows, "I waited patiently for the Lord; and He inclined to me, and heard my cry. He brought me up out of the pit of destruction, out of the miry clay; and He set my feet upon a rock making my footsteps firm. And He put a new song in my mouth, a song of praise to our God; many will see and fear, and will trust in the Lord."

Ephesians 4:32 tells us, "And be kind to one another, tender hearted, forgiving each other, just as God in Christ also has forgiven you."

It's just not about forgiving but also about being kind and loving to each other. Trust may have to be built again but we can forgive and give it all to God to handle. He can mend any heart as long as were willing to walk with Him. God never stops loving or forgiving us so how can we decide to do something that He Himself would never do?

Jeremiah 31:3 says, "I have loved you with an everlasting love, I have drawn you with loving kindness."

Psalms 103:1-3 says this, "Bless the Lord oh my soul and all that is within me bless His Holy name, bless the Lord oh my soul and forget not all His benefits: who forgiveth all thine iniquities, who healeth all thy diseases."

Ephesians 1:7 says, "In whom we have redemption through His blood, the forgiveness of sins according to the riches of His grace."

Joseph is a powerful example to us of many things. His story represents forgiveness, love, strength, courage, and the power of God. How God can take something that was meant for evil in our lives and turn it all around to the Glory of God. This story should bring much hope to you if you feel you are in a pit or have ever been in a pit. God will take you out of that situation and bring you into His full plan for your life and let it be used for the Glory of God.

Faith – Forgiveness – Peace

In Luke 7:37-50 we read a story that we all can learn from. The story goes as follows:

Jesus was dining with a Pharisee at his house. They are sitting there with each other and in walks in this woman. This woman was known at that time "As a sinner." Somehow this woman knew that Jesus was at this Pharisee's house and went there on her own to see Him. She didn't wait for an invitation. Probably because she knew deep down she wouldn't have gotten one.

So she comes into this house and stands at Jesus' feet weeping. She then begins to wash Jesus' feet with her tears and wipes her tears away with her hair and kisses His feet. Then she opens her alabaster box of perfume that she had brought with her and begins to anoint His feet with this perfume.

The Pharisee then says to himself "If this man were a prophet He would know who and what sort of person this woman is who is touching Him, that she is a sinner." Jesus then turns to Simon and begins to tell this story about two debtors. It goes as follows: "A certain money lender had two debtors. One owed five hundred denari and the other fifty. When they were unable to repay he graciously forgave them both, which of them therefore will love him more?" Simon answered and said, "I suppose the one whom he forgave more." And he said to him "You have judged correctly." Jesus then turns towards the woman and says to Simon "Do you see this woman? I entered your house, you gave me no water for my feet, but she has wet my feet with her tears and wiped them with her hair. You gave me no kiss; but she since the time I came in has not ceased to kiss my feet. You did not anoint my head with oil, but she anointed My feet with perfume. For this reason I say to you, her sins, which are many, have been forgiven, for she loved much; but he who is forgiven little loves little." And He said to her "Your sins have been forgiven." Jesus then says to the woman "Your faith has saved you; go in peace."

This story is amazing. This "sinful" woman of that day had an amazing amount of humility, courage, and strength. We can learn quite a bit from this story.

1. The Lord's love for us is not measured by how many sins we have committed. He isn't concerned with what we have done. He already shed His blood for our forgiveness. He just wants us to Love Him with everything we are. To offer up all of ourselves to Him.

2. We learn about not judging others. We are not to look at others as though we are better and not quite as "sinful."

3. This woman brought this costly perfume to anoint Jesus. This alabaster box of perfume represented 1 years' worth of wages – and she gave it unto her Lord. Even the disciples said "Why this waste – this perfume could have been sold at a high price and the money given to the poor." This woman gave her very best to Jesus. Are we willing to give our very best unto our Lord?

4. We also learn humility, courage, strength, and love by her actions. She didn't care what others thought about her. All that mattered to her was Jesus. Despite the situation or circumstances that were surrounding her she didn't let others opinions of her sway her form what she came there to do.

5. Lastly again we have forgiveness through Christ. It does not matter how many sins we have committed, they are all under His blood.

Psalms 103:12 reminds us of this last point, "As far as the East is from the West so far has He removed our transgressions from us. Just as a father has compassion on his children so the Lord has compassion on those who fear Him."

Another key in this story is found in verse 50, which says, "And He said to the woman your faith has saved you, go in peace."

The word "peace" means, "A state of mental or physical quiet or tranquility: calm. Freedom from mental agitation or anxiety."

The Lord instructed her to go in her new found peace which is from Him. Her sins were forgiven and remembered no more. We will never forget every wrong choice we have made, but we don't need to define ourselves by those choices. We are only defined and refined by our loving, faithful, and forgiving Father. We have been given a beautiful free gift: Forgiveness and Peace. We need to accept His gifts to us and move on. Move on towards Him and serving Him with all that we are. Serving Him with our whole body, soul and mind and loving Him completely and wholly. Also to remember that as were forgiven and don't deserve it we need to freely forgive others.

You Are What You Think

When I went to our youngest son's conference his teacher was telling me about how shy he still was, but that he was slowly coming around. She said some of the parents have said that "He is cute, but so shy." Also, that it has been said in front of him. She told me that she asked them not to say that, because she didn't think he should hear it. She then told me story about a little girl in one of her classes who was very little for her age. Whenever people would see her they would say, "Oh, you're so tiny, and so cute." Eventually after a while when people would meet this girl, she would say what her name was, followed by "I'm tiny." This had been said so much around her that she identified herself as "tiny." She told me this because she didn't want our son to do the same thing. Now this little girl most likely already felt smaller than the other kids, but with everyone saying it, it reinforced it in her mind and she ended up defining herself by her size.

From that story we learn how important it is to watch what we say to others. It's also important to be very careful what we say or think about ourselves. Proverbs 23:7 says, "For as he thinketh in his heart, so is he."

When I was in high school people knew I was from, what they called back then, "a broken home," and that my real father was not in my life. I remember someone once saying, "I was illegitimate," and I was constantly reminded of my darker skin (being half Mexican), growing up. Now while all that was the truth, I let it sink into my thoughts, and I let it become the focus of who I was, and who I wasn't. There were other factors along the way that contributed. In my mind I was a looser, because I was fatherless and had to dark of skin. My attitude turned very negative about myself.

I eventually took a wrong turn in my life. I chose to basically walk away from God. I chose to do what I wanted. I was tired of being hurt, used, and abused. I was only making things worse, because now what I was doing was a slap in Gods face, and it was on purpose. I never verbally said to God, "I don't want to lean on you and trust you, please don't help me," but my actions reflected it. I tried to fix myself the way I wanted, and to be honest sin is fun, or no one would do it.

You see my thoughts were on my pain, my hurt, and myself. I wasn't willing to give it all to Him to handle and heal. Then the thoughts of guilt came. In my mind I was no good, not loveable, and not worthy.

Thank God His thoughts are higher than ours, in every way. Isaiah 55:8 says, "For my thoughts are not your thoughts, neither are your ways my ways declares the Lord. For as the heavens are higher than the earth so are my ways higher than your ways and my thoughts than your thoughts."

Take a moment now and think on an average, "What are my thoughts about?" "Am I mostly thinking negative about life, others and myself?" "How do I really see myself?" "Do I really see myself, for who I really am in Christ's eyes, or have I let others and circumstances dictate what I think about myself?"

Paul in 11 Corinthians 10:4-5 says, "We need to bring every thought into captivity and bring it unto obedience in Christ." If we are constantly in a state of jealousy, worry, and pride – how do these things line up with the word of God, and His will for our lives? If our children were constantly coming to us saying negative things about others or themselves, we couldn't take it. We as parents want the best for our children. We want them to feel great about whom they are. If they continued to do such destruction to themselves, most likely they would lead a miserable life. They would never see themselves how us as their parents see them.

God love for us is the same, but much higher. God says in Genesis He created man in His own image, in the image of God He created them. 1 John 3:1 says, "Behold what manner of love the Father has bestowed upon us, that we should be called the sons of God: therefore, the world knoweth us not because it knew Him not."

Philippians 4:8 says, "Finally brethren whatever is true, whatever is pure, whatever is lovely, whatever is of good report, if there is any excellence and if anything, worthy of praise, let your mind dwell on these things. The things you have learned and received and heard and seen in me practice these things and the God of peace shall be with you."

Life is hard a lot of times. We all can get caught up in thinking negative, worrying about finances, our children, our marriages, careers, etc. When we though fully give God our whole lives, which means body, heart, soul, and mind and let Him be the center of it all, only then will we have peace. For every worry you will ever have, or every negative thought you think about yourself or others, there is a word, a positive word and answer from God in the Bible. When we can come to the place of really knowing who we are in God's eyes, we will never again think negative about ourselves again. How do we get to that point you may ask? The answer is found in the word of God. Go there and find out what God thinks about you, and how much He loves and values you.

Spirit Or Flesh Walking

What does it mean to walk in the spirit, how do we know if we are truly walking in the spirit? How many situations come up in one day that we have to make a choice? That choice to "walk in the flesh" or "walk in the spirit?" What are the consequences for our choices?

I chose to walk to "walk in the flesh" for many years. I chose to do what I wanted when I wanted. Since I was walking in the flesh I wasn't going forward I was just going around in circles, and at times downward. My thinking was these "worldly things" were fun, they were making me happy, and in some things I even tried to justify my behavior. I tried to make it seem to myself like what I was doing wasn't all that bad. Actually I was running, running from God. I wanted to do things my way, and my attitude was nobody is my boss!! Not the right way to live when you have been a Christian since the age of 7, but it is the truth.

Turn to Galatians 5: 16- 25. "But I say, walk by the spirit, and you will not carry out the desire of the flesh. For the flesh sets its desire against the spirit, and the spirit against the flesh: for these are in opposition to one another, so that you may not do things you please. But if you are led by the spirit, you are not under the law now the deeds of the flesh are evident, which are: immorality, impurity, sensuality, idolatry, sorcery, enmities, strife, jealousy, outbursts of anger, disputes, dissensions, factions, envying, drunkenness, carousing, and things like these, of which I forewarn you just as I have forewarned you that those who practice such things shall not inherit the kingdom of god. But the fruit of the spirit is love, joy, peace, patience, kindness, goodness, faithfulness, gentleness, self-control: against such things there is no law. Now those who belong to Christ Jesus have crucified the flesh with its passions and desires. If we live by the spirit, let us also walk by the spirit. Let us not become boastful, challenging one another, envying one another."

Clearly this is an outline for what is "flesh" and what is "spirit." What we should and should not be doing. Since we are not perfect, we can expect to mess up. Even at times, "royally blow it." The Lord though says in Lamentations 3:19-24, "Remember my affliction and my wandering, the wormwood and bitterness. Surely my soul remembers and is bowed down within me (or humbled in me). These I recall to my mind, therefore have I hope. It is of the Lords mercies that we are not consumed, because His compassions fail not. They are new every morning: great is thy faithfulness. The lord is good unto them that wait for Him, to the soul that seeketh Him."

Also 1 John 1:9 says, "If we confess our sins, He is faithful and just to forgive us our sins, and to cleanse us from all unrighteousness."

So, since we know we are going to "blow it," because we're not perfect, we have the assurance that we have forgiveness, and His mercy is ever constant and present in our lives.

The next time we are about to open our mouths or we start thinking the wrong thing, we need to quickly realize what we're doing. We need to get out of our "flesh" and walk in the "spirit." A lot of times it's a second by second process, but once were accustomed to recognizing it we can get out of it quicker and easier. God says He sent His Holy Spirit to be a comforter and teacher to us. The Bible warns us not to grieve the Holy Spirit in Ephesians 4:30. We can grieve the Holy Spirit by not walking in the spirit, His spirit. We need to always be sensing His presence in our lives, and when at times He's prompting us to say or do something, and when He's prompting us not to say or do something.

Really Knowing God

What does the Lord mean to you? If He chose to walk away from you what would you miss? What would be different in your life? Think also to a good friend you have. Think of all the time that has been spent getting to really know each other. How at times you each other can even finish each other's sentences. You know each other's likes and dislikes, strengths, and weaknesses. Maybe even for some at the beginning, before the friendship even took off, you knew about one another, but you didn't really know them. Now think if that person said to you "I don't want to be your friend anymore," and they were gone. What had taken you years perhaps to build on was now over. How would you feel? This person who knew you so well and who you loved, was now out of your life.

Jeremiah 1:5 tell us, "Before I formed you in the womb, I knew you, and before you were born, I consecrated you. I have appointed you a prophet to the nations."

Matthew 10:30 says, "But the very hairs of your head are numbered."

Imagine knowing someone so well that you know the exact number of his or her strands of hair. Think to that verse in Jeremiah. Before He formed us, He knew us! Wow! If anybody truly knows us, it is God. How well do we know Him? We can know a lot about Him, but how well do we really know Him? If He were to say goodbye to us, what would we notice right away missing? Would we only be concerned with our salvation and where we were to spend eternity?

If we were to lose that friend we loved, our minds would go back to some great times. Times when they had really been there for us, made us laugh, listened to our problems, were even there to give us a hug, smile or kind word.

How close is the Lord to us, or should I say, how close are we to Him? How much of a personal relationship do we really have with Him? The Bible gives us many definitions of how God feels for us. He is called our Father, He says we are His friends, He is our strength, our joy, our rock. It goes on and on. So, He is many things to us, and loves us. How do we feel about Him? What words do we use to describe Him to others or even to ourselves? How often do we tell others about Him? Just as having that great friend here on earth, we know it involves a lot of time, but it's worth it for us. How much time do we spend with the Lord? Do we spend enough time just to get our requests in or are we truly spending quality time with Him? In order to have a growing two-way friendship here on earth we both must give. With God He already gave us His best, and He continues giving, but how much are we giving? Are we truly giving in order to get or just truly giving?

Ordinary People = Extraordinary Things

How many of us have thought to ourselves, "How could God ever use me?" Sometimes when we look at ourselves all we see is our weaknesses and failures.

I have been in that same boat. I guess I truly believed I was no one special. I have no college degrees, I don't work outside the home, and I don't really have any specialized skills. Then the night I prayed a short, but heartfelt prayer my life changed.

When the Lord spoke to me about this group, I immediately obeyed but was not sure how it would all fit together. The Lord though has been faithful to me, and I believe His blessing is upon each one of us as His children.

At Christmas time my family always reads the birth story of Christ. I love the story because it's not a fictional story like we read our children, it is real! I believe that story should be read often so we don't ever forget what Christmas all is about.

The story of our Savior being conceived and brought into this world is found in Luke 1 & 2. Picture a woman named Mary loving God, and just being a woman. Someone who is engaged to be married and thinking of all the plans to be made for her wedding and starting their lives together, and wham!! Here comes Gabriel the angel. Wow, what a day that must have been for her! In Luke 1:34 Mary herself asks the angel "How can this be, since I am a virgin?" The angel's response was simple "The Holy Spirit will come upon you, and the power of the Most High will overshadow you." He then goes on to tell her in verse 37 of the same chapter that "For nothing will be impossible with God." Mary then responded "Behold, the bondslave of the Lord; be it done to me according to your word." Wow, what an incredible woman. To know that this was going to take place and that her whole life was going to change. She didn't even try to refuse or argue with the angel. Now we know why she was the chosen one to do this.

Mary was the chosen one to give birth to our Savior, and what a miracle it all is. I think of Mary, and then think what if that would have been me? I would have been to say the least a little freaked out!! Mary then begins in verse 38 to accept the will of God in her life and receives what He has just told her. She then goes to her cousin's house who is also pregnant with John the Baptist, and her cousin Elizabeth says in verse 45, "And blessed is she that believed: for there shall be a performance of those things which were told her from the Lord." Mary then praises God for what is to come. She is rejoicing in vs. 48-49 for Him choosing her.

Now we will never compare to what Mary did. The Messiah already has been born, crucified and rose again. However, we can do great things for God. Each of us has been created for God's purpose and plan. Our main purpose is to love and worship Him above all other things, but then it doesn't stop there. He wants us to go out and fulfill the mission He has predestined for each of us.

Don't let society tell you that you are not worthy because you don't have a bunch of titles behind your name, because God has the best title for you, and that is you're His daughter! In verse 37 we read that nothing is impossible to God. Since He planted Jesus in her womb, then He can do anything. Also, don't get caught up the thinking that I did, "That I'm no one special, God can't use me." I am, by society standards, no one truly exciting or special, but in Gods eyes I' am special and very much loved, just like each of you. We are not here by accident or mistake.

The Lord has taught me many things through being involved in this ministry. When we think we do not have any special skills that is when He pulls out everything He put in us to begin with. Something we never knew existed, something maybe we never wanted to do, but now we find out that we love it and can't imagine ever doing anything else.

I'm not saying we are all "Marys." Her job was the greatest there was. I look at her and think, what a remarkable woman. She trusted the Lord, even when she didn't really understand how, and He blessed her, and through her the world had a Savior. Whatever God calls you to do, it will bless others, and believe me when I say you will also be blessed. What if Mary denied what God told her. Naturally He could have done it if He wanted, but what if she fought Him? The same is true of us. Whatever God wants us to do is important. If we deny it, or walk away from it because of fear, insecurity, etc., there will be people affected by our turning away. We're in effect saying, "No" to those people God had in mind for us to show Christ's love to. The job God has in mind for each of us is designed in such a perfect way for us, and that is why He has chosen us to do it. So, this Christmas if you read this story, be reminded of what a miracle God performed, and how He used an ordinary woman by the world's standards, but highly extraordinary in God's eyes. Think to yourselves and know He loves you as much as He loved Mary and He wants to use you. Remember when you're in His hands there's nothing to be afraid of, only excited about!

Follow Me

When we accepted the Lord into our hearts and lives, we acted in faith. We fully believed God sent His son and had him die on the cross for our sins. We also believed He rose on the third day, and because of that we were saved from an eternity in hell. We knew at that moment we were someday going to spend eternity with our heavenly father Jesus Christ. What an act of faith that took, choosing to believe in something we had never seen but knew we were saved. We put our eternal souls into the Lord's hands.

Why is it then for some of us we have such a hard time totally surrendering our lives here on earth to God's plan and purpose for us? Why do we still want to control our own lives and make our own decisions? We depend too much on ourselves, and what we want and don't want. It's as though were saying, "Ok Lord I trust you with my eternal life, but not my earthly one." We knew at the moment we accepted Christ was because we needed and wanted Him in our hearts and lives. We trusted that he heard us and saved us but why not every day, in every situation? Christ did not just die on the cross, so we could have forgiveness, go to heaven and then say to us, "Ok go on now, I'll find out how your life went when you get to Heaven."

He wants our lives to always reflect Him. He wants to guide us and give us an abundant life. John 10:10 says, "The thief cometh not, but for to steal, and to kill, and to destroy. I am come that they might have life and have it more abundantly." Jeremiah 29:11 says, "For I know the plans I have for you" declares the Lord, plans to prosper you and not harm you, plans to give you hope and a future."

God's word tells us He has good plans for us, not to hurt us. There should be no hesitation in us saying, "Lord take my whole life, my plans, my thoughts and do what you want." Who are we to think we know more than God? We are only here because He created us. He gave us life! When we try to handle our own lives, we are in effect saying, "I don't trust you Lord and I think I can do it better." That sounds harsh but its realty.

What is amazing is the disciples gave up everything to follow Jesus. Matthew 4:18-22 says, "And walking by the sea of Galilee he saw two brothers, Simon who was called Peter, and Andrew his brother casting a net into the sea; for they were fisherman. And He said to them, "Follow Me, and I will make you fishers of men." And they immediately left the nets and followed Him. And going on from there He saw two other brothers, James the son of Zebedee, and John his brother, in the boat with Zebedeee their father, mending their nets; and he called them. And they immediately left the boat and their father and followed Him." Matthew 9:9 says, "And as Jesus passed on from there, He saw a man, called Matthew, sitting in the tax office; and He said to him "Follow Me!" and he rose and followed Him."

These men immediately rose to their feet and followed Jesus. They had no idea what was in store for them. They gave up their careers and left their family members to follow Jesus. The word "Follow" in the dictionary means, "To come or come after and in the same direction." Jesus wants us to follow Him- to go in His direction not him in our direction.

I encourage you to not only look to him regarding your salvation, but to look to Him for everything. Remember His plans for us are good, better than we could ever imagine. We have nothing to fear by giving Him total control over our lives. 11 Timothy 1:7 says, "For God hath not given us a spirit of fear, but of power, and of love and of a sound mind."

It's a walk of faith that we must take, but also an exciting journey. Hebrews 11:6 says, "And without faith it is impossible to please Him, for he who comes to God must believe that He is, and that He is a rewarder of those who seek Him." The disciples didn't always fully understand everything, but they continued to follow Him. We are as well not always going to understand and foresee things, but that's the exciting part! Look at what the disciples would have missed had they not "Followed" the Lord. They gave up everything for Him and I guarantee you that they never regretted their choice. Let's not miss out on what God wants to do through us and for us to accomplish His will.

Spend Time With Me

For any relationship to work, thrive, and grow there needs to be "time together." Time for two people to share their thoughts, desires, get advice and to just listen.

Imagine someone in your life your close too. Maybe it's your spouse, relative or a close friend. Now imagine if they were constantly coming to you and telling you all their problems, but they wouldn't be quiet long enough for you to respond. Imagine them being in your presence talking, crying, etc., and then they turned around and left. Perhaps you would run after them calling them by their name because you wanted to help, but they just kept going as if they couldn't hear you. You would be left standing there thinking, "If they would have only let me respond I could have helped them." How frustrating would that be?

A lot of times that's how our prayer lives are. We pray long enough to get our requests in and then were done. We walk away. Imagining yourself earlier standing there as the person you loved, left. That's what God feels like. I imagine Him saying, "Wait, wait I have an answer for you. I want to help, please hear what I have to tell you."

What ends up happening is it becomes a "one-way" relationship at that moment. God does want us to pray to Him and to give Him all our burdens, but He also desires more.

Psalms 55: 22 says, "Cast your burden upon the Lord and He will sustain you; He will never let the righteous to be shaken."

Hebrews 13:6 says, "The Lord is my helper I will not be afraid what shall man do to me."

The Lord wants and instructs us to give Him all our cares and that He will help us. He though also wants to speak to us and for us to listen to Him.

Matthew 11:15 says, "He who has ears to hear let him hear." He commands us to use our ears to listen to His voice. Maybe you're not sure to know how to hear the Lord. Isaiah explains in chapter 50 verses 4-5, "The Lord God has given me the tongue of disciples that

I may know how to sustain the weary one with a word. He awakens me morning by morning, He awakens my ear to listen as a disciple. The Lord God has opened my ear; and I was not disobedient, nor did I turn back."

God will awaken our ears to hear Him. We ~~just need~~must be willing and obedient to fully seek Him and His voice. When we come into the Lords presence speaking ~~to~~unto Him He wants to respond back to us~~, it's just often we~~. We are in too much of a hurry though a lot of times to just be still and listen.

Proverbs 4:20 says, "My son attend to my words; incline thine ear unto my sayings. Let them not depart from thine eyes; keep them in the midst of thee." The Lord wants to speak to us all the time. When He does speak to us though we are to obey His instruction. So, the next time you're in prayer take some time and ask the Holy Spirit to speak to you. You will be amazed and astounded at what real conversation is like with our Lord. He wants to continually speak to us. It's us who doesn't give Him a chance to be heard, because we are too busy, and at times too selfish with our time. Just as no relationship can work without two people listening to each other, we can't survive without hearing Gods words to us through His word, and through His voice.

Who Do You Worship?

When we decide to follow Jesus we make the choice to follow all His commands, or at least we should. Some of us are willing to do all that He commands like pray, love others, give our time to the Lord's work, but when it comes to our money, we cringe! We just can't seem to let go of our pocket books very easily.

The second commandment though says, "You shall not make for yourself an idol, or any likeness of what is in heaven above or on the earth below or in the water under the earth. You shall not worship them or serve them; for I the Lord your God am a jealous God." Money is something that helps us pay our bills, purchase food, provide shelter etc., but God is the source. He is the source for everything. He tells us in James 1:17 that, "Every good thing bestowed and every perfect gift is from above, coming down from the father of lights with whom there is no variation, or shifting shadow."

Deuteronomy 8:18 says, "But you shall remember the Lord your God, for it is He who is giving you power to make wealth, that He may confirm His covenant which He swore to your fathers as it is this day."

Everything we have comes from God. He gives it to us. He also gives us the power and ability to make wealth so we can have the things we need. We though tend to look at our jobs and paychecks getting so caught up in ourselves that we forget that He made it happen for us.

The second commandment easily relates to our money issues as well. Like I stated earlier, we are willing to give up everything to follow Jesus, except our pocketbooks. When that happens it is because we have placed too much trust in our money. We then don't tithe or even give to others. We end up placing too high a value on our money. We become dependent on it, we safeguard it. What ends up happening is that it becomes an idol in our lives. We place it above God. We may not think it's an idol, but when our trust is more in our money than God then it has become an idol. We definitely need money to make it in this world but we need to trust in God first, not just what our bank account says.

God doesn't need our money. When He asks us to tithe it's a matter of obedience of giving our "first fruits" back to Him. It is all His anyways because all things come from Him. Let's also remember He is asking for 10% not 90%. He could have reversed it, but He didn't.

Malachi 3:8-12 says, "Will a man rob God? Yet you are robbing me! But you say; "How have we robbed thee? In tithes and offerings. You are cursed with a curse; for you are robbing Me, the whole nation of you! Bring the whole tithe into the storehouse, so that there may be food in My house, and test me now in this," says the Lord of hosts, "If I will not open for you the windows of heaven, and pour out for you a blessing until it overflows, Then I will rebuke the devourer for you, so that it may not destroy the fruits of the ground, nor will your vine in the field cast its grapes" says the Lord of hosts, "And all nations will call you blessed, for you shall be a delightful land" says the Lord of hosts."

This verse is the only verse that says, "Test me." He tells us He will bless us so much that we are overflowing in blessings. That He will make sure the enemy doesn't get a hold of it! What more assurance could we need from Him that He will take care of us?

Maybe you have never thought money was an idol in your life, but ask yourself these questions:

1. Why don't I tithe or tithe regularly?

2. What do I trust more in, God or my money?

3. Do I believe God will fully take care of my needs if I tithe?

4. Do I want to ever or continue to rob God?

Tough questions I know but God tells us what to do. Are we doing it? Psalms 49:6 says, "He who trust in his riches will fall, but the righteous will flourish like the green leaf." God wants us to trust Him for everything, because He promises He will meet every need we have and more. Philippians 4:19 says, "And my God shall supply all your needs according to His riches in glory in Christ Jesus." We need to obey the Lord fully in everything and trust He will meet the needs of His people like He has promised, and He will!

Do Not Be Afraid Or Ashamed

I have never been in fear or persecuted for sharing my faith and for that I'm thankful and blessed. We live in a free world for the most part where we can say anything, good or bad.

In Daniel 3 King Nebuchadnezzar was upset that Shadrach, Meshach and Abednego did not worship the golden image that he set up. He told them that if they continued to not worship the image he would throw them into a "burning fiery furnace." The three of them however continued to say they would not worship the Kings god. They said that the God they served was able to deliver them out of the "burning fiery furnace," but that if He chose not to deliver them that they still would not worship the Kings god. They would only worship and serve their God.

This infuriated the King and he had them bound and put into a furnace. The furnace was heated seven times hotter than normal. The fire was so hot that it slew the men who were ordered to put them in there. The King at one point looked inside the furnace and was amazed, because he said he saw four "loose men." That no one was bound and they were walking around in the midst of the fire and were not hurt. The fourth person that the King said he saw was in the form of the Son of God.

King Nebuchadnezzar then commanded them to come out. When they came out he and all the princes, governors, captains and the Kings counselor's saw that they were not bound. Their clothes were not burned, not one hair of their head was singed, and they didn't even smell like fire. The King then realized that their God was the one true God and that God had sent his angel to save His servants. He then changed the decree and said that if anyone spoke against the God of Shadrach, Meschach, and Abednego they would be cut in pieces, and their houses would be ruined because their God was the one true God. After this these three men were then promoted.

There are many other stories of people being persecuted for their faith, but that didn't stop them. In Acts we read about Paul being beaten and put in prison several times. God though repeatedly provided means of miraculous circumstances to get him out of prison and provide for him. Paul continued serving God regardless of what came his way because he knew he had a mission to fulfill.

1 Thessalonians 2:4 says, "But as we were allowed of God to be put in trust with the gospel, even so we speak; not as pleasing men, but God, which trieth our hearts."

Romans 1:6 says, "For I am not ashamed of the gospel of Christ; for it is the power of God unto salvation to everyone that believeth; to the Jew first and also to the Greek."

Shadrach, Meshach and Abednego took a stand for God and would not back down even though they knew they were facing being burned to death. They knew God had the power to deliver them, but they didn't ask for it. They chose God above all things, even their own lives. Being put into a furnace would be a horrible and painful death to go through, but God delivered them and the Kings heart was changed.

We do not face that in the United States, at least not yet. We have to stand for Christ no matter what others will think about us. We are to please God in all things, not men. We cannot be ashamed of the gospel. We are here to win souls for Gods kingdom that's our mission. We cannot do that though if we are afraid of what others will think of us. God is always with us and just like those three men, God always wins by our standing for our one true God.

Welcome Home

How many times have we said, "I'm not worthy"? How many times have we continued to visit our "past" in our minds and then feel so shameful and condemned because of our mistakes? When we recall those mistakes, we can feel more "unworthy" and "un-loveable." At those moments we can feel such condemnation that we can't get past it, and at times we can't accept God's forgiveness and love towards us because of our shame. We think "I'll come to God when I get myself cleaned up" or "I'll come to God when I'm no longer making these mistakes anymore." We can even think that God will love us more when we are a little more "presentable" in His sight.

In Luke 15:1-24 we read the story about the prodigal son. The word "Prodigal" means "Addicted to wasteful expenditure, as of money, time, or strength; extravagant."

This son took his half of his father's estate that was entitled to him and left to a far and distant place, and in our term of words he "blew it all." He spent his money on everything and anything he could. He used that money on sinful and shameful things. Then when he realized he was "broke" a severe famine broke out, and he had no money to buy food. So out of desperation he goes to a stranger for help who then sends him to go help with the pigs! So, there he was in the middle of the pigs and he found himself hungry. He was so hungry that he was willing to eat what the pigs ate, but no one would give him anything. The Bible says that when he came to his senses, he said his fathers hired men ate better than this and that they have plenty to eat.

He then realized that he needed to repent and go home. He even said that he felt so "unworthy" that he shouldn't even be called his father's son anymore, and that he should be as one of his father's hired men. He felt a lot of shame and guilt at that moment, but in his heart he was sorry and wanted to repent to God and his father.

So, he decided to go home and the Bible says that he was yet a ways off and yet his father saw him coming and felt compassion for him. He ran, embraced and kissed him. It's as though his father was outside watching for him to come home. He was welcoming him with all the love a father has for his son. The son then humbled himself and repented to God and his father, and said, "I'm no longer worthy to be called your son." The Bible says the father called his slaves and told them to quickly bring the best robe, ring and sandals and for it all to be put on his son. The father goes on to say, "His son who was "dead" is now alive and who was "lost" is now found."

This father instantly forgave his son and restored him to his family. The son came home with no money and a "past," but he also came with a repentant heart towards God and his father, and both forgave him. His father then brings out the best of everything for his son and rejoices that his son is home. No questions asked. No hesitation.

This story should give us much joy and peace, because it's about our father and us. We all have been the "prodigal" son or daughter at one time or another. We have all turned to our own ways and have done what we wanted regardless of the price to others or us. We do though have a father who is "looking" for us with His arms outstretched waiting to take us again into His arms blessing us with all His best. He rejoices when we are looking to Him and not to our past, to our shame and guilt. When we repent and humble ourselves our father is always there for us. We are not worthy on our own based on our actions, because we all fall short. We are though "worthy" because we are His sons and daughters, and that qualifies us for everything He wants to do for us. It's not about what we have done, no matter what it is or how many times we have done it. It's about how much love, forgiveness, and grace that is available to us at any time.

We can't let our past or pride get in the way of us "going home" to our Father. He's looking and waiting for us. He wants to lavish everything He has on us because His love for us is endless, and so is His forgiveness.

Walking In Love

It's so easy to say, "I love you." The phrase is used so much and loosely that we tend to not really walk in the true meaning of it. It is three simple words, but it gets "tossed" around so much that it doesn't mean what it's supposed to truly mean. We can say, "I love you a thousand times a day to someone, but our actions many times do not back up those 3 simple but powerful words.

Saying "I love you" is so common place anymore that I really wonder if people realize what they are saying. 1 Corinthians 13:4-8 is a passage used a lot in marriage ceremonies, but it's something we need to frequently look at and see if when we say I love you our actions are reflecting Gods definition of love. God's word says "love is patient, Love is kind, and is not jealous. Love does not brag and is not arrogant, does not act unbecomingly; it does not seek its own, is not provoked does not take into account a wrong suffered, does not rejoice in unrighteousness, but rejoices with the truth, bears all things, believes all things, hopes all things, endures all things."

This is a clear definition of what love is and what love is not. John 15:12 tells us, "This is my commandment that ye love one another, as I have loved you." John 15:17 also tells us, "These things I command you, that ye love one another." Jesus is not asking us to love one another. He is not casually saying "Well if you feel like walking in love go ahead, but if you don't then you don't have to." He is Commanding us to love one another and to love one another as He loves us.

Romans 12:9-21 says, "Let love be without hypocrisy, abhor what is evil, cling to what is good. Be devoted to one another in brotherly love, give preference to one another in honor; not lagging behind in diligence, fervent in spirit, serving the Lord, rejoicing in hope, preserving in tribulation, devoted to prayer, contributing to the needs of the saints, practicing hospitality. Bless those who persecute you; bless and curse not. Rejoice with those who rejoice, and weep with those who weep. Be of the same mind toward one another; do not be haughty in mind, but associate with the lonely. Never pay back evil for evil to anyone. Respect what is right in the sight of all men, if possible, so far as it depends on you, be at peace with all men."

This passage takes us a step further on how to walk in love towards others. As Christians we are "One body in Christ" and we need to act that way. If we were to cut our finger, we would take our other hand to clean the wound and put a band-aid on it. We wouldn't let our finger go "un-nursed." The same is true of us. We need to always be that "helping hand" to others, and to walk in love towards the body of Christ and to non-believers. To walk in the true meaning of love with our spouses, children, family members, and our friends.

Jesus was mistreated so many times, but He always walked in love and most important forgiveness. He never quit giving and meeting the needs of others. We are to, as well, emulate Christ and strive more and more to walk in "Godly character" in every situation, and with everyone. We may not always approve of others actions, but we can always walk in love.

When we say, "I love you," we need to realize what we are saying. We need to always back up those words with actions. Actions that are Christ like and that define what true love is.

Not Mine But Thine

When we are raising our children we want the best for them. We want them to grow up as strong, healthy, mature and responsible adults. We do our best to teach them everything that is good, and most important what is the true way according to God's word, and hope that one day it makes a difference. There are also those times when they want to do things that are not beneficial to them and we must say "no" to them. At those moments it becomes our will over their will, and they do not always see it as a good thing, but in time we know it will be for their own good.

For us as God's children it can be the same way. He knows what is best for us even when we can't always see it clearly. We want our own way, because we think we know what is best and we can have such a difficult time conforming to His will. We like to be in control, to know what is coming at all times and we even tell ourselves that we have everything under control. When that happens though eventually the "bottom seems to fall out," and what started out as everything appearing in control and good has ended up in disaster.

Even with our children they have to learn "the hard way." We as adults also go through the same thing. Society is not much help in this area either for they encourage "Self-reliance" which often leads to not asking anyone for help including God. We feel the need to be self-reliant, because if we can't make things work within ourselves for some reason we feel it shows our "inadequacy." Yet following in this thinking leads us to at some point experiencing burn out and possibly even major mistakes. We then find ourselves becoming mentally drained and physically tired.

In Luke 22:42 we read about Jesus in the garden of Gethsemane. He was there praying on the night before He was to be crucified and He prayed "Father if Thou be willing remove this cup from me; yet not My will, but Thine be done."

Jesus knew that He had to die on that cross for mankind, but I'm sure He dreaded it. You must remember even though He was the Son of God, He was still flesh and blood, and being crucified was an extremely long and painful death. He also knew it was going to be beyond painful, but He prayed "Your will be done" and then followed through with God's will, and because of that choice we have eternal life and forgiveness of all our sins.

Our prayer should always be the same that Jesus prayed. "Yet not My will, but Thine be done." Too many times we pray for our will to be done when the focus of our lives should always be God's will above anything else, for what do we really have to give up compared to Jesus? The answer is, <u>nothing that matters</u>. Our time, wants, desires should always conform to Him and His will and not ours. We need to continually make sure our lives reflect the will of God and not our own will. We are to remember that it's just not about doing whatever "purpose" God has for us, but also about our daily routines- our daily habits. It's about seeking and worshipping God daily and letting the love of God shine through us towards others.

We need to remember that we cannot and were not meant to live our lives with "us" as the focus, for when that is the case that is when the bottom seems to eventually fall out. Even Jesus' life was not about "Himself," but it was about "serving" others and doing the will of His Father and our lives should and need to be the same way every minute of every day. Think for a minute if Jesus would not have followed the will of God, we would be "eternally lost." In the same way if we do not follow the will of God for our own lives we will never have the meaning and purpose that our lives were created and meant to have. We will not be able to affect those around us for Christ. So, start now living your life according to His will and not your own!!

Your Hired!!!

Whenever a person wants to apply for a new job they must fill out an application. Sometimes business' will go one step further and require a resume and or a background check. They want to know that the person they are thinking of hiring is a capable, knowledgeable and experienced person for the job. They want to know when that person starts that position they will be an asset to their company.

In God's "business" though, there are no background checks or resumes that are required, and much less experience. Take Saul of Tarsus for example. He was a persecutor of the church and the Lord used him in a powerful way.

In Acts 8:3 we read, "But Saul began ravaging the church, entering house after house; and dragging off men and women, he would put them in prison."

In Acts 9:1 we read another account of Saul "Now Saul still breathing threats and murder against the disciples of the Lord, went to the high priest and asked for letters from him to the synagogues at Damascus, so that if he found any belonging to the Way, both men and women he might bring them bound to Jerusalem."

Saul of Tarsus was, in our words of today, "bad to the bone." People were terrified of him. They were in fear of their lives, but the Lord knew that he was truly not "bad to the bone." The Lord had a plan all along for Saul, and He would use Saul in an amazing way.

Saul started his day out most likely like any other day. His mission was to persecute the church. So, one day he was on his way to do just that, and then all of a sudden the Lord literally "blindsided" him. Jesus struck down Saul with a bright light and said unto him "Saul, Saul, why persecuted thou me?" Saul answer was, "Who art thou Lord" and the Lord said back "I am Jesus whom thou persecutest; it is hard for thee to kick against the pricks." Saul by then is terrified and says, "What do you want me to do"? Jesus then answers him and says, "Go into the city and it will be told to him what he must do."

Now the other men who were with Saul heard Jesus' voice, but didn't see anything. They then had to help Saul into the city because of him being blinded. While there he didn't eat or drink anything in those three days, but did pray. During that time, he had a vision that a man named Ananias would come to him, put his hands on his face and that he would see again.

The Lord also at this time tells Ananias to go to Saul who is expecting him, because he had a vision. Important thing to know is Ananias knew who Saul of Tarsus was. I imagine at first, he was scared. Maybe in fear of his own life. He was, though, obedient to what the Lord had asked of him which is amazing. The Lord told Ananias that Saul was a chosen vessel for the Lord. That he was meant to bear the name of Jesus before everyone. When Ananias went to Saul he did as the Lord instructed him to, and prayed over him and Saul's eyesight was restored. Saul was also filled with the Holy Ghost and baptized. When he had regained his strength, he went out to preach the name of Jesus and to testify that He was the Son of God.

This story is so incredible, and yet it gives us hope. If the Lord could use a man whose main focus was to kill Christians He can and will use each of us. Our past has no hold on us in God's eyes. He does not require a "background check" or even a "resume." It does not matter to God what we have done in our past. Absolutely we need to repent and seek the Lord and His path for our lives, but our past does not limit our future in God's plan.

Jesus took a man and in three days completely changed his life forever, for the better. He also changed his name from Saul to Paul. The Lord used that same passion that Saul had for persecuting the church and turned it around and made his mission for Christ his passion. Think to how many books of the Bible we have because of Paul's writings. Paul was absolutely sold out to Jesus, no matter what the cost to him.

This story of Paul shows us how much God loves us and definitely has a plan for us. We need to as Paul says in Philippians 3:13 "Brethren I count not myself to have apprehended; but this one thing I do, forgetting those things which are behind and reaching forth unto those things which are before."

Paul knew that how the Lord changed his life was truly a gift. He pressed on each day as if it was his last to win souls for Jesus, and the Lord was always with him.

In each of our lives we all have a "past." Things that we wish we could forget. What we fail to always remember is that God created us for His purpose, and His plans do not change. We have total forgiveness of our sins through the shedding of His blood, and the Lord says He no longer remembers our sins. So why do we? He is always on our side regardless of our "past," and He wants to use each of us. When you have those moments and think, "God could never use me, I have made too many mistakes." Think of this story of Paul and let it remind you that with God all things are possible, and that if he used Paul He will use you.

Are you willing to be used?

Will you be sold out to Him?

Will you let Him be your passion?

Answer The Call

Romans 8:28 says, "And we know that God causes all things to work together for good to those who love God, to those who are called according to His purpose." Romans 8:31 says, "What then shall we say to these things? If God be for us who is against us?"

From these two verses we can assuredly understand no matter what we are facing God is bigger than any circumstance that comes before us. That God is always with us, and on our side. Now upon knowing this truth imagine if you had a dream concerning Bin Laden. Let's say you had a vison in which you were to go find him, lay hands upon him and pray for him. You though were not allowed to bring anyone with you. You had to go alone. What would your fist thought be?

In Acts 9:10-18 we read a similar but true story. There was a devout man named Ananias. Ananias had a vision that he was to go to the "Known terrorist" of that time. He was to go to this persecutor of the church and pray for him, because he was a chosen vessel for the Lord. The Lord also told this man Saul as well that Ananias had a vision of him as well coming. Ananias I'm sure at first was both nervous and unsure. He tells the Lord that he knows how this man has done evil to the saints and has the authority to persecute all believers. The Lord though tells Ananias that Saul will be used for God, and so he agreed to go. When Ananias saw Saul, he called him "Brother Saul" and then prayed for him. Saul's vision was restored, he was baptized and then started his journey of being used by God.

Hebrews 13:6 says, "The Lord is my helper, I will not be afraid what shall man do to me?" Isaiah 12:2 says, "Behold God is my salvation I will trust and not be afraid, for the Lord God is my strength and song and He has become my salvation." In Acts 9:10 it says that "The Lord said "Ananias" and Ananias said, "Behold I am here Lord." Then obeyed the call. The Lord equally is always "calling us," but will we choose to answer?

There will be times where we may not understand everything God wants us to do at first, but we must fully trust in Him. Maybe it's the fear of the unknown or yet even the fear of the known. It requires faith and trust in every situation- but we must choose to say, "Here I am Lord." God's word tell us He is our helper so why be afraid? We many never have to go to the Bin Laden's of this world like Ananias had to, but we will have to do something for Him. Regardless of whatever God asks of us to do He will be there for us. He will never ask us to something and then quit on us. Ananias was faithful and walked in faith and trust in God, and God didn't allow any harm to come to him.

Hebrews 11:6 says, "Without faith it's impossible to please Him." We know that God is our helper and that He is always with us and for us. The question is will we walk in faith and trust in God and say "Behold I am here Lord" when He calls us?

Seek Him Not His Hand

If you were to go to a bookstore today you would be amazed at how many books there are regarding parenting. There are books from "Trying to get pregnant" to "Raising teenagers" plus many more.

Having that first child can be very overwhelming for some and to have that extra help is very helpful. I myself also researched many books while pregnant for the first time to gain some sort of wisdom. I knew that my child would eventually be in my arms and although I knew a natural mothers instinct existed I still felt I needed to gain some more wisdom and knowledge than what I felt I had at the time. Having these books available to me gave me much needed insight and some confidence needed.

King Solomon also understood this concept of wanting and needing understanding and wisdom. Solomon was the son of King David who was a very Godly man and King and Solomon I'm sure learned so much from his father about the role of being a King. However when King David died and Solomon was the next King he was humble enough to realize that he needed God's help.

In 1 Kings 3:5-14 we read about Solomon's humble request to God. God had in a dream appeared to Solomon and asked him what He could do for him. Solomon responded to God with humility and asked that God would give him an understanding heart to judge the people, so that he could discern between good and bad. This request pleased God and God responded back with that because Solomon did not ask for long life, or riches for himself, or for the life of his enemies but asked for understanding to discern judgment He would bless him all the way around. God told Solomon that He would give him a wise and understanding heart and that He would give him riches and honor. God also said that there would never again be any man like him. Solomon could have had the attitude of that "I've arrived". He could have been very proud and done things his way. After all, he was the King. King Solomon though actually described himself as "I am but a little child, I know not how to go out or come in." He through this truly humbled himself and cried out to God for what we all need, wisdom.

No matter who we are or where we are in life we will always need the Lords counsel. None of us will never so call "arrive" so much that we will not need Gods wisdom and direction. What each of us needs to do is do as King Solomon did that day and rid ourselves of our pride and ask God for the direction and wisdom needed to do things the way He would want us to do them. The Bible tells us that "My people are destroyed for a lack of knowledge" which in effect serves to remind each of us that we can never have too much wisdom or knowledge.

Proverbs 4:5 says to us, "Get wisdom, get understanding forget it not; neither decline from the words of my mouth. Forsake her not, and she shall preserve thee: love her and she shall keep thee. Wisdom is the principal thing; therefore get wisdom and with all thy getting get understanding."

Proverbs 3:5-7 says, "Trust in the Lord with all thine heart, and lean not unto thine own understanding. In all thy ways acknowledge Him and He shall direct thy paths. Be not wise in thy own eyes: fear the Lord and depart form evil."

God through these verses is instructing us to turn to Him for everything and to gain His wisdom and then to follow through on what it is He is telling us to do. James 1:22 says, "But be ye doers of the word and not hearers only deceiving your own selves."

God shows us through this story of Solomon that when we seek Him and not just His hand that is when He is pleased. That if each of us would humble ourselves before the Lord and seek Him He will answer us. We also through this story are reminded that no matter who we are we are nothing without God and His wisdom. He also reminds us that He is about blessing His people because of His great love for us. So whatever your position is in this world start today to ask God for the wisdom, understanding and knowledge that you need to effectively to do whatever it is you do and remember to honor God with all you are and have.

I've Had Enough

How many times have you found yourself saying, "I've had enough Lord?" I have said that many times because I felt like I just couldn't take one more thing- and then it seemed like more just kept coming.

Elijah in the Bible also said "Enough" to the Lord. In 1 Kings 19:1-8 we read the story of his coming to the "end of his rope." Jezebel had sent word to Elijah that she was going to kill him because she was angry that he had killed 450 prophets of Baal. Elijah after hearing that took off running for his life and went to the wilderness. He sat down under a tree and said, "It is enough; now O Lord, take my life, for I am not better than my fathers." Now here is a strong man who loved the Lord and had given up. Elijah though had just proven that his God was the one true God through the fire of the wet altar, had the prophets killed then went and prayed for rain and God sent the rain to a place that was in dire need of rain. This man had had an incredible day with the Lord, now here he is scared saying "enough."

Elijah decided he just wanted to at this point die and wanted Gods help. He decided to go to sleep (most likely hoping he wouldn't wake up) and God comes to his rescue with an angel. An angel who appears to Elijah saying, "Arise and eat." Elijah looks and sees a bread cake baked on hot stones and a jug of water. He decided to eat it then proceeded to lay back down. The angel comes again and says, "Arise, eat because the journey is too great for you." So, Elijah got up ate and drank and that meal strengthened him for 40 days and 40 nights as he went to Horeb the mountain of God.

Many times, we can feel like we've had enough and we're done. We're just too tired and perhaps scared. God though says to us constantly "Rise up." He tells us in John 14:6 "I am the way, the truth, and the life." Isaiah 40:24-31 tells us, "He giveth power to the faint, and to them that have no might he increaseth strength. Even youths shall faint and be weary and the young man shall utterly fall: but they that wait upon the Lord shall renew their strength; they shall mount up with wings as eagles; they shall run and not be weary, and they shall walk and not faint." Isaiah 41:10 says, "Fear thou not; for I am with thee be not dismayed: for I am they God., I will strengthen thee; yea I will help thee: yes, I will uphold thee with the right hand of my righteousness."

Elijah knew the power of God- he had just experienced the hand of God on his life. He though got scared, ran and gave up. He didn't even ask the Lord for help, just for help to die. Perhaps we would have done the same thing. Perhaps we already have. This story teaches us many things:

1. God never gives up on us.
2. He listens to us wine and complain.
3. He's always right on time with his provision and its always abundant.
4. God is always on time- at times not early but never late.
5. God never gives us more than we can handle.

God tells us we are going to face trials in this world, but that He is our strength. He is our provider because of His love for us. When trials and hard confusing times arise in our life we need to look up to God. We can't allow ourselves to give up and to focus too much on our circumstances. We need to constantly be seeking Him and watch how He delivers us and at the same time strengthens us. We need to remember that nothing is too difficult for the Lord. To remember the ways, He has always provided and showed up for us in the past and know that He will again be there for us, forever and ever.

Do Whatever It Takes

Have you ever known someone who was truly determined to do something? Someone determined enough not to give up, regardless of how hard or impossible the situation appeared to be? Most likely that person achieved their goals because of their determination.

In Mark 2:1-4 we read about the determination of some men towards a paralytic man. The story goes as follows: Jesus was in Capernaum preaching to such a large crowd surrounding Him that people couldn't even get to the door to get in to hear Him. There then came some men carrying a man who needed healing because he was paralyzed. As these men got closer they saw, because of the large crowd they couldn't make their way to Jesus. Now at this moment they could have given up. Said they were sorry he wasn't going to get his healing, because they just couldn't get in and quit. They decided though through determination to go one step further and not give up. Together they tore the roof off piece by piece eventually being able to lower their friend directly down into the sight of Jesus and he was healed. The Bible does not tell us how long it took or even if they had any tools available to them, however what is evident is they were determined to not let anything stand in their way and they didn't. These men were willing to go the distance for this man regardless of how much time it took, and how many obstacles were facing them. Because of that this man was restored to great health not only outside, but inwardly as well.

Another important lesson to learn from this story is these men never asked for a thank you or recognition. They were not found bragging or boasting on what they had done, because these men they knew it wasn't about them, but about their friend and Jesus who healed him.

Galatians 6:2 tells us to, "Bear one another's burdens, and thus fulfill the law of Christ."

1 John 3:16-18 says, "We know love by this, that He laid down His life for us, and we ought to lay down our lives for the brethren, but whoever has the world's goods, and beholds his brother in need and closes his heart against him, how does the love of God abide in

him little children, let us not love with word or with tongue, but in deed and truth."

The men in this story are true examples of what God's word tells us to do. There are so many needs in this world, and equally so much we can do to help. We must be willing to take a closer look at those around us, and their need and a way we can help. Not to just wait for someone to come to us but for us to be aware. To be determined to help, and not give up despite how impossible or time consuming it may be. The Bible says we are to "bear" or "carry" each other's burdens (needs) because that is one way we show God's love to others and we are to do it humbly and willingly. To help out of sincere love for others and not out of the hope of personal or public recognition. Not only willing to help if it does not "put" us out too much, but because of the love of God within us. We need to also remember that with God He is the One who always sees when we help others and will bless us accordingly. For when we help others it is too be unto the Lord Jesus Christ not for public accolades.

I admire the courage, love, dedication, and determination of these men for what they did for that man as I'm sure the man who was healed would also agree. Imagine the thankfulness this man had felt as he witnessed what lengths his friends were willing to go for him. Imagine this man lying on a stretcher hearing all their challenging work taking place and imagine the thoughts that ran through his mind. His friends that day were determined to get him to Jesus and by their actions these men are still bringing others to Christ. May we all have those same qualities to help those in need around us. May we never give up so that others may be brought into the presence of Jesus Christ, and be restored not only physically but internally as well.

Ask And Receive

"What would you like?" is a question we usually ask people around the holidays or when a birthday is approaching. The reason we ask this is because it helps give ideas as to what that person would like, which in turn helps us in our shopping for that person.

Sometimes as children of God we think we can't ask for things because it's selfish. We think to ourselves, "Well God knows what I have need of and He'll give it to me when He wants to." While that statement is true, God does know what we have need of, but He still tells us to ask.

Matthew 7:7-11 teaches us this principal. "Ask, and it shall be given to you; seek, and you shall find; knock, and it shall be opened to you. For everyone who asks receives, and he who seeks finds, and to him who knocks it shall be opened. Or what man is there among you, when his son shall ask him for a loaf, will give him a stone? Or if he shall ask for a fish, he will not give him a snake, will he? If you then, being evil know how to give good gifts to your children, how much more shall your father who is in heaven give what is good to those to ask Him?"

1 John 5:14-15 reads, "And this is the confidence which we have before him that, if we ask anything according to His will, He hears us. And we know that He hears us in whatever we ask, we know that we have the requests which we have asked from Him."

My children have asked me for many things over the years, and I'm thankful they feel comfortable enough to do so. My answer may not be what they always want to hear, but as their parent I have to decide if it's the right thing at the time or not. There are times when I say "Yes" and times I say "No." Then there are those moments when I say "Yes, but not right now." My heart always wants to give them the desires of their hearts, and I'm thankful they ask because how else would I have known?

Our Father in heaven also wants to give us the desires of our heart. He, though, has the perfect timing for all things because He sees things we can't and never will. His answer to us will be the same answers as we give our kids. He truly wants to give us all that we ask but at times, He can't. He knows what is good for us and what is not. He knows that if He were to answer "Yes" to something for us, down the road we would have realized that either we needed to wait, or that it would have been better to have an answer of "No" to us. He answers us accordingly to His perfect will for us, but we still receive an answer.

Our Father tells us to <u>ask</u> because He will answer us and wants to give us the desires of our heart. If at the time we don't receive the answer we were wishing for we have to realize that He does have a perfect plan for us. Just as parents on earth try to fulfill (within boundaries) their children's desires, so does God. He wants us to ask and to seek Him for everything.

I have known people who wouldn't think to ask God for things. They have thought either it was selfish, or that God had more important things to handle than their requests. For me personally I go to our Father about everything because I know there is nothing wrong with asking, and I believe our Heavenly Father is waiting for us to ask. I can tell you honestly, at first I was not used to going to Him for everything, even small things. Now I know that when I call upon His name <u>for anything, any need big or small or just a desire</u>, He hears me and always answers me.

Look at it this way, for us to be a child of God and have Him living inside of us, didn't <u>we have to first ask, and didn't He answer us</u>?

The Perfect Calm

Think back to a time in your life when you were really struggling. A time when everything seemed like it was never going to end. Think honestly to yourself for a minute, did you feel all alone? Although you knew logically that God was with you, did you still feel like He wasn't there? Did you feel that maybe God wasn't aware of you? When that "storm" though was over, you more than likely realized that He <u>was</u> there with you or you wouldn't have made it through, right?

There's a similar story in Mark 4:35-40 it reads as follows, "That day when evening came, He said to His disciples "Let us go over to the other side" leaving the crowd behind, they took Him along, just as He was, in the boat. There were also other boats with him. A furious squall came up, and the waves broke over the boat, so that it was nearly swamped. Jesus was in the stern, sleeping on a cushion. The disciples woke him, and said to him "Teacher, don't you care if we drown?" He got up, rebuked the wind and said to the waves "Quiet! Be still!" Then the wind died down and it was completely calm. He said to His disciples, "Why are you so afraid? Do you still have no faith?"

Picture in your mind for a moment this happening with <u>you</u> in that boat. Here you are in the boat with Jesus planning to go to the other side because He asked you to. You're in the boat talking with your friends and Jesus is nice and cozy asleep on a cushion. You're going along and everything seems great and calm – your waiting to get to the other side. Then from out of nowhere a fierce storm blows in. The boat is filling up with water. You find yourself drenched and you start to panic. You look over at Jesus who is still sleeping. He is not woken by the waves coming in the boat and drenching Him. You by this point are scared and you wake Jesus up angrily out of fear and ask Him "Teacher don't you care if we drown?" Jesus then gets up rebukes the wind and waves and in an instant a perfect calmness takes over. Jesus then looks at you and says "Why are you so afraid? Do you still have no faith?"

How appropriate for us in those times when we feel like were "drowning" and we feel like He's "asleep." We cannot, however, be governed by our feelings, only by what the Lord tells us. His truth.

Remember also that Jesus was the one who said, "Let's go over to the other side." When they got into that boat, they were going with Him like Jesus asked of them. They were going in expectation of getting to the other side.

There are times when God tells us to do something and we are obedient. We are excited and happy to go on the journey with Him. Then a "storm" breaks out in our lives and we immediately think the worst. We feel God has suddenly left us and that he doesn't care what we are facing. Then at the perfect moment when we need him to intervene, he comes in calming the "storms" and we continue on the journey.

Jeremiah 23:23-24 reminds us of His nearness to us. "Am I a God who is near." Declares the Lord "And not a God far off? "Can a man hide himself in hiding places, so I do not see Him?" declares the Lord. "Do I not fill the heavens and the earth?" declares the Lord."

Philippians 4:6 says to us, "Be anxious for nothing, but in everything by prayer and supplication with thanksgiving let your requests be made known to God."

We have to continually remember that our Father is always with us and always aware of us. When we feel were in that "storm" we need to realize who is at the "front of the ship." He's the one who gets us to where we need to go. He's not "shaken" by the storms as we learned in the book of Mark.

The disciples in the boat that day, had Jesus in the flesh with them. They had heard him preach and perform many miracles, and yet they doubted. For us, we have Jesus living inside of us. He's always with us. There's nothing He isn't aware of in our lives, and nothing He can't handle.

Hebrew 13 tells us, "The Lord is my helper I will not be afraid what shall man do to me."

So, the next time a so called "storm" blows your way, know He's with you and providing a way through it. Take a seat on a "cozy cushion," and watch how He calms the storm to a "perfect calm."

Small But Deadly

One of the smallest parts on our bodies is our toes- yet they hurt the most when "stubbed." Stubbing our toe can quickly bring us to our knees, literally.

Another one of our smallest body parts is our tongue. Even though it is small it can produce extremely large wounds to others.

In James 3:8-12 we learn about how deadly our tongues are. "But no one can tame the tongue; it is a restless evil and full of deadly poison. With it we bless our Lord and Father and with it we curse men, who have been made in the likeness of God; from the same mouth come both blessing and cursing. My brethren, these things ought not to be this way. Does a fountain send out from the same opening both fresh and bitter water? Can a fig tree, my brethren produce olives, or a vine produce figs? Neither can salt water produce fresh."

How true is the verse is for each one of us? To know that when we are hurting men who are in Gods image with our words is a devastating thought. Now that we know what the problem is with our tongues, let's look at some instructions from God on how to control our tongue.

Ephesians 4:29-32, "Let no unwholesome word proceed out of your mouth, but only such a word as is good for edification according to the need of the moment, that it may give grace to those who hear. And do not grieve the Holy Spirit of God, by whom you were sealed for the day of redemption. Let all bitterness and wrath and anger and clamor and slander be put away from you, along with all malice. And be kind to one another, tender hearted, forgiving each other, just as God in Christ also has forgiven you."

Proverbs 15:1-4 tells us this, "A gentle answer turns away wrath, but a harsh words stirs up anger. The tongue of the wise makes knowledge acceptable, but the mouth of fools spouts folly. The eyes of the Lord are in every place, watching the evil and the good. A soothing tongue is a tree of life."

It is so easy to get caught up in our emotions and let hurtful words fly out of our mouths. Those words end up being words we wish we could take back, but we cant. It is much better to walk away at that moment and come back later so as not to say anything we would regret.

The instructions in Ephesians should continually be on our minds. As much as we need to not say hurtful things, we also need to be lifting others up. Perhaps it's a good idea to start taking a daily inventory of the words that we speak each day. Look back at the day and ask yourself, "Did I lift anyone up my words or were my words stirring up anger?" Then think, "What can I do better tomorrow with the Lords help because I want my words to glorify Him."

Our mouths are not tamable on our own. We need the Holy Spirits help, continually. We are though responsible when we know God's truth and we don't apply it. We cannot blame others for their words and use that as an excuse for our words. We have to take a moment and think, "Alright, I'm angry right now but I refuse to allow my tongue to speak poison." It is a difficult thing but God is telling us we can do it with His help. Each word we speak should be soothing and edifying to others. After all, are we not to treat others as we want to be treated? Sometimes that has to come even when we are being hurt ourselves by other's words.

No Excuses

Have you ever been around someone who seems to have an answer for everything? It doesn't matter what you say, they have a response. If they are giving the right answers though, it doesn't bother us. It's when they "think" they know but in reality they do not have a clue. That's when it upsets us, right?

Moses had an encounter with God. An encounter that showed him that God had an answer for all of his questions and excuses.

In Exodus 3 we read about Moses' encounter with God. Moses was out one day doing his usual routine, that of tending his fathers-in-law sheep. Moses was married and had one child, and was busy doing his responsibilities. Then, out of nowhere, Moses sees a burning bush and goes to look at it, and that's when he heard God speaking to him. God told Moses that He wanted him to go to Egypt and bring His people out of the affliction they were under. You would think at this point Moses would have thought to himself "Ok, this is God telling me this, and I better just do it right away." Moses though is like us in a lot of ways. He likes to ask questions! Moses had five things to present to the Lord.

1. Moses says to God: "Who Am I that I should go to Pharaoh, and that I should bring the sons of Israel out of Egypt?"

2. Moses then says: "Behold, I am going to the sons of Israel, and I shall say to them, "The God of your fathers has sent me to you!" they may say to me, "What is His name?" What shall I say to them?"

3. Moses then asks: "What if they will not believe me or listen to what I say? For they may say "The Lord has not appeared to you."

4. Moses then pleads: "Please Lord, I have never been eloquent, neither recently nor in time past, nor since thou hast spoken to thy servant; for I am slow of speech and slow of tongue."

5. Moses' last request: "Please Lord, now send the message by whomever Thou wilt."

Of all of Moses' concerns God had an answer to each one. God in a nutshell told Moses that He would be with him. That He was the God of Abraham, Isaac, and Jacob. God told Moses that if the people did not believe him that he would be able to perform signs and wonders before their eyes with his staff. God also told Moses that He would be with him all the way and that He would be Moses' mouth and that He would direct him on what to say, also that Moses' brother would be going with him to also be a mouthpiece for him.

You see, God always has all the answers. We do not need to argue with God. We don't need to try to figure everything out. We just need to be obedient to what He's asking us to do. Moses was like us today. Like I stated earlier, he was married had a child and a job. He was being responsible with what he had in front of him, but God needed him. Moses was the chosen one to lead those people out of captivity. He was created for that purpose. Once Moses heard all of Gods answers, he did choose to up root his family and went to do what God had asked of him.

You see, God is not interested in our excuses or our own reasoning. We are on this earth to fulfill the mission that we were created for, not for what we have created. We are not here for our desires or ourselves.

1 Peter 4:10 says this to us, "As each one has received a special gift, employ it in serving one another, as good stewards of the manifold grace of God."

Colossians 3:24 tells us, "Whatever you do, do your work heartily as for the Lord rather than for men, knowing that from the Lord you will receive the reward of the inheritance."

When Moses gave the Lord all his concerns and so called excuses, notice that not one of them had to do with his family schedule or his time. Moses loved God and honored God and took his family with him to do God's will. You see each one of us was bought and paid for by Christ's death. We have forgiveness of sins eternal life with Christ and most of all His love.

We are to take every opportunity to show that love of Christ to others and to do whatever He asks of us.

I Corinthians 6:19-20 tells us this, "Or do you not know that your body is a temple of the Holy Spirit who is in you, whom you have from God and that you are not your own? For you have been bought with a price; therefore glorify God in your body!"

We do have a responsibility to our families, job etc., but those are choices we made. We were put here for whatever missions the Lord has for us to accomplish. He has given each one of us a gift – a gift especially designed for us and we are to glorify Him by using that gift.

So, the next time you try to make excuses as to why you shouldn't do what God wants you do, know He will always have an answer back to you. Once you let go of your excuses and go in His direction, that's when your life glorifies the Lord.

Which Way Are You Running?

How many times have you heard or said yourself "You can't run from your responsibilities?" For parents that statement is used a lot in a child's life. Children know they have certain duties to fulfill. Some may include chores around the house, cleaning their rooms, laundry and even getting their schoolwork done. Children have seen that their parents are aware if they are doing their personal responsibilities or not. They have repercussions for not doing what their parents have assigned for them to do. They can't "hide" when a duty is not performed, they can't run. Parents will see that dirty room, see the chores not done, and even that report card. It would have been better for them at the time to just do what was required of them.

The story of Jonah is about the same issue, running from responsibility, and from God. The story of Jonah is in the book of Jonah and it is only four chapters long. A quick story but a major lesson for us to heed.

The story of Jonah is quite simple. Jonah was told by God to go to a city called Nineveh and preach to them and to warn them of their wickedness against God. Jonah though decides to disobey and run from God. Jonah decides to board a boat to another city in an attempt to "flee." While on this boat a fierce storm broke out. A storm that was life threatening to all on board. The men aboard that boat knew that Jonah was the cause of this storm because of his own admission of guilt. Jonah then tells them to throw him overboard and that by doing that the storm would cease. So they did this at Jonah's request, and the sea grew calm again.

Jonah then was swallowed by a large fish and lived inside of this fish for three days and three nights. While he was inside the belly of this fish he started to pray. He repented of his ways to the Lord and then the fish vomited him out. Jonah at this point did go to the city of Nineveh and warned them like the Lord had asked him to. The city and its entire people repented of their ways and because of this the Lord saved them from destruction and the wrath of God.

One may ask, "Why did it take him three days to repent?" "Why wouldn't he just obey God's voice and commands?" Perhaps the question should be turned around to ourselves. How many times has God told us to do something even something simple and we "run"? The "running" usually though lasts longer than 3 days in most cases. How much brokenness do we inflict on ourselves before we let go of "ourselves" and return to the presence of God?

We cannot hide from God, ever! He always knows exactly where we are. When Jonah boarded that boat he probably thought to himself, "I'm safe in this boat and I can get away from going to Nineveh."

When God calls us to do something He will not let us give Him the so called "slip." He has chosen each of us for a particular assignment and no amount of running will change that.

God chose one man to help deliver 120,000 people from destruction. Now that's not to say each of us is called to help deliver 120,000 people but even one person is just as important to God as 120,00. Whatever the Lord is asking of us big or small He will equip us with every tool we need. We cannot "run" from our responsibilities to our God. Each of us was created for something – something that glorifies God. There is no use in "running" or trying to "hide" from God because He is always "aware" of us and where we are. We need to be obedient in everything He asks of us – everything!

Deuteronomy 28:1 tells us this, "If you fully obey the Lord your God and carefully follow all His commands I give you today the Lord your God will set you high above all the nations on earth."

Think of all that Jonah went through because of his "running" and disobedience. Ask yourself this important question, "Am I running from God or am I running towards God?" If you're running away from God then turn back and run towards Him.

Sit and Listen

How many times on holidays do we over-do it by taking on the whole responsibility of the meal preparation ourselves? People are flocking in happy to be there talking, and we're "at the stove." We don't have time to socialize because we have to "serve" dinner. Then when dinner is finally done were exhausted and upset that we didn't have more "hands" helping us.

There's a story in Luke 10:38-42 that relates to this issue a bit. The story is about two women - one named Martha and her sister Mary. Martha knew Jesus was in "town" and welcomed Him into her home. Now picture Martha trying as fast as she can to "whip up" something for Jesus to eat. During all this she realizes her sister Mary isn't helping her and she is irritated- after all she is trying to "serve" Jesus and she isn't getting any help. She sees Mary in the other room sitting at Jesus' feet learning from Him. Martha can't believe it, she can't believe she's doing all the work and here's her sister sitting on her "tail."

Martha says to Jesus "Lord do you not care that my sister has left me to do all the serving alone? Then tell her to help me." Jesus then replies to her "Martha, Martha you are worried about so many things; but only a few things are necessary, really only one, for Mary has chosen the good part which shall not be taken away from her."

Now since we do not know what happened next in the story, it causes us to wonder, how did Martha react to Jesus' words to her? Some might even ask, "But are we not to serve?" "Was Martha wrong in serving Jesus?" "Wasn't Mary wrong for not helping her sister?"

The lesson to be learned is that Jesus said Mary had chosen the good part, which shall not be taken away from her. At that moment it wasn't about "service" it was about just being with Jesus, sitting at His feet, and learning.

So many things can happen in a single day that keep us from not taking the time to "sit" with Jesus. We are so busy with all of the "things" we have to get done that we end up "missing" Him. Mary knew when He came in she was not going to miss this opportunity to listen and learn from her Lord, even if her sister got upset with her.

You see, Jesus was the most important thing that day and she had to be with Him, really be with Him.

On the flip side, we have to remember as well that we are called to serve others, which is worship unto the Lord. We just need to remember that we cannot replace "being at His feet" with "service." To not allow ourselves to get so caught up in service that we don't spend time with Him.

Think also to this analogy. The Bible says Martha welcomes Jesus into her home. She's busy preparing food for him (an act of service). Then she's upset because she's not receiving any help, and then Jesus backs up Mary.

Perhaps we could look at it also like this. We once welcomed Jesus into our hearts and lives, our "home."

Maybe though, over time, we have gotten so busy serving Him that we have quit coming to His feet as often as we once did. Then we stop and say, "Lord why aren't you helping me, don't you see I need your help?" Perhaps Jesus is asking you to please choose Him and to make time for Him. He is supposed to be the most important person in our lives.

There needs to be a balance between service and sitting at His feet. Jesus first wants you. He wants your heart, mind, body, soul, and time. Time just for you and Him. Even in the midst of serving, are you sitting at His feet? Or are you too busy with your serving that you cannot set aside regular time with your Lord, at His feet?

Back At You!

How many times do we look at others and their actions and judge them? Why is it that we are we so quick to bring out others faults when perhaps we have done or are doing the same thing?

Let's imagine you're sitting with a person talking and judging someone you know and suddenly, the lights go out. Instantly it's as if a movie projector turns on and on the wall, is your life playing out in front of you. Only this "movie" is bringing out not only every wrong choice you have ever made, but also every thought you have ever had cross your mind!! Imagine sitting there with your friends and your whole life is being "viewed" and when the lights come back on everyone is looking at you in disgust and unbelief. The things that you had just gotten done judging someone else on were the same things that you yourself were guilty of. Your friends then look at you and say, "You are no better than so and so - look at what you have done!"

What a horrible thought that is! To think that our whole lives could be revealed for others to know is too much to handle. The point is, we all have made wrong choices in our lives so who are we to judge others? We also need to remember that thankfully we have God's forgiveness when we don't deserve it, and so does everyone else.

Matthew 7:1-5 say this, "Do not judge lest you be judge. For in the way you judge, you will be judged; and by your standard of measure, it will be measured to you. And why do you look at the speck that is in your brother's eye, but do not notice the log that is in your own eye? Or how can you say to your brother," Let me take the speck out of your eye and behold the log is in your own eye? You hypocrite! First take the log out of your own eye, and then you will see clearly to take the speck out of your brothers eye."

The old saying, "back at you" is profoundly true, and God's word tells us that by how much we judge others it will come back to us.

Romans 2:1-2 also says to us, "Therefore you are without excuse, every man of you who passes judgment, for in that you judge another, you condemn yourself; for you who judge practice the same things, and we know that the judgment of God rightly falls upon those who practice such things."

If you really take a moment to think about it, it is a pretty scary thought to think that because of your judging others you will be judge according to how much you judge. We are by nature judgmental people. However, by being God's children, we are to reflect Him and to love others. We are not to judge others by their mistakes and choices, for even we need the shedding of Christ's blood for our sins. We would never be on our way to Heaven if He hadn't have done that for each of us so our sins could be forgiven, and that is what we need to remember.

So, the next time your quick to judge, think of yourself. Think of the choices you have made, and how much you have needed forgiveness and mercy from God. Think about that, and give your love and mercy to others, and not your judgment.

Turn Back

Have you ever heard the saying "There are no atheists in a foxhole"? The message is simple in that sooner or later we all will get to the point where we cry out to God for help in our desperate situation. How many though after getting that help never praise God for what He did? How many cry out for help, get what they want, and walk away?

The story of the Ten lepers found in Luke 17:11-19 is similar to this very thing. The story is, "And it came about while He was on the way to Jerusalem, that He was passing between Samaria and Galilee. And as He entered a certain village, ten leperous men who stood at a distance met Him; and they raised their voices saying, "Jesus, Master, have mercy on us!" And when He saw them, He said to them, "Go show yourselves to the priests." And it came about that as they were going, they were cleansed. Now one of them, when he saw that he had been healed, turned back, glorifying God with a loud voice, and he fell on his face at His feet, giving thanks to Him. And he was a Samaritan. And Jesus answered and said, "Were there not ten cleansed? But the nine where are they? Was no one found who turned back to give glory to God, except this foreigner?" And He said to him, "Rise and go your way; your faith has made you well."

You see, these men were in a desperate situation and they knew Jesus could heal them. They cried out to Him for help and were healed. The amazing thing is that they also went on faith in that they had to act before they were cleansed. After this amazing event only one man came back to glorify Jesus for His healing, and his soul was made well also.

Jesus desperately loves each of us and wants to meet our every need. He though wants us to praise, honor and glorify Him in everything because He is everything.

Psalms 34:1-8 tells us this, "I will bless the Lord at all times; His praise shall continually be in my mouth. My soul shall make its boast in the Lord; the humble shall hear it and rejoice. O magnify the Lord with me and let us exalt His name together. I sought the Lord and He answered me, and delivered me from all my fears. They looked to

Him and were radiant, and their faces shall never be ashamed. This poor man cried and the Lord heard him and saved him out of all his troubles. The angel of the Lord encamps around those who fear Him, and rescues them."

The next time you cry out for your Master to rescue you, know that He will. Also, though, remember you must continually let praise and worship be on your lips. Do not get what you wanted, then walk away and do your own thing so to speak. Run to Him, fall on your face before Him glorifying Him, not just for what he did for you but for who He is. Turn back the blessing that He gave you into praise and adoration for your Master.

Hurry – Come Down!!

When I was a young girl my cousins and I liked to climb trees in the backyard. We would love to see who could get to the top and shake the treetop first. Many times my Aunt would come out and tell us to get down from those trees. She said we were up too high and because of that it was dangerous. We would agree and start coming down a few branches and then she would go in. As soon as we saw her go in we would race up to the top again. Looking back now it was dangerous and she was right, we needed to get down when she asked us to.

There's a story about a man named Zaccheus in Luke 19:1-10 who also climbed a tree. However his story is much different than that of mine. His story goes as follows, "And He entered and was passing through Jericho and behold there was a man called by the name of Zaccheus: and he was a chief tax- gatherer, and he was rich. And he was trying to see who Jesus was, and he was unable because of the crowd, for he was small in stature. And he ran on ahead and climbed up into a sycamore tree in order to see Him, for He was about to pass through that way. And when Jesus came to the place, He looked up and said to him, "Zaccheus, hurry and come down for today I must stay at your house." And he hurried and came down, and received Him gladly. And when they saw it, they all began to grumble, saying, "He has gone to be the guest of a man who is a sinner." And Zaccheus stopped and said to the Lord, "Behold, Lord half of my possessions I will give to the poor, and if I have defrauded anyone of anything, I will give back four times as much." And Jesus said to him, "Today salvation has come to this house, because he, too, is a son of Abraham. For the Son of Man has come to seek and to save that which was lost."

Here is a man who for as much as we know had everything (according to the world's standards) and yet he was still missing something - Jesus. He was very wealthy and yet he was curious about Jesus and took extreme measures to see him. Jesus comes looks up at him and tells him to hurry and come down so He could go to his house. Imagine what Zaccheus was thinking. His immediate reaction was one of total obedience. He got completely out of that tree and received Jesus. He knew this was a moment he wasn't going to miss and he embraced Him with all that he was.

So many times in our lives we also are in the "tree" so to speak. Except for us, when Jesus is calling our name, we don't come down completely. We might come down a few branches and then we are back up again just "observing." Perhaps we're afraid to come completely down because of what we think it will cost us. Look though at Zaccheus. He wasn't under any judgment or condemnation from Jesus, but was a changed man just from being in the presence of Jesus. He said of his own free will that if he had cheated anyone out of anything in the past due to his job that he would pay it back four times more. This man and his character was changed Jesus didn't make him say that.

John 3:16-18 tells us this, "For God so loved the world that He gave His only begotten son that whoever believes in Him should not perish but have eternal life. For God did not send the Son into the world to judge the world, but that the world should be saved through Him. He who believes in Him is not judged; he who does not believe has been judged already, because he has not believed in the name of the only begotten Son of God."

Jesus came in to this world to seek and to save what was lost not to judge or bring condemnation. Each person needs to ask himself or herself this one question, "If I died tonight where would I spend eternity?" If that is a question that you do not have an answer for then you have a choice to make. The choice is will you accept Jesus into your heart and life and let Him be the center of your life? If you want to make that choice then pray this prayer "Father I believe you sent your son Jesus Christ and had Him die on the cross for me. That through the shedding of His blood I have forgiveness of all my sins. I believe that He rose on the third day so I could have eternal life. I ask you now to forgive me and to cleanse me of all my sins because I'm a sinner and I need you. Come into my heart and be the Lord of my life. Thank you for your free gift of salvation and thank you for loving me. In Jesus name I pray amen."

Perhaps you have gotten out of the tree before and yet you find yourself climbing back up those branches and you want to come down again, fully. Re-commit your life to Christ and start walking closely with Him again. He hasn't forgotten you and you haven't done anything that could make Him not love you. His love for us never changes.

Christ is there calling each person's name to get out of the tree that they are in so that He can be a guest in their "house." The question is do you want to be high in a tree just seeing and observing Jesus or do you want to get completely down and have Him in your "house" forever? He desperately loves you and wants to be with you forever. "Won't You Hurry And Come Down?"

It's All From Him

(My son has given his permission to tell this story about a lesson he learned, which relates to what God's word tells us.)

One year during baseball season my son was what you would call "In a slump." He had gone through ¾ of the season hitting very well and was at the top of his game. Then suddenly he wasn't able to hit the ball at all. Many people tried to offer their advice and tips to get him hitting again but nothing worked. He was getting extremely upset and was quickly losing his confidence, which broke his fathers and mine heart.

One day after yet another "hit-less" game, I had a talk with him at home. I asked him what he felt the problem was and if there was something he could do different. He couldn't think of anything to try which frustrated him even more. Then the Lord visited us in his room and led us to the answer. I asked him if he felt he had become a little arrogant and prideful in himself because of his natural ability. If that also perhaps God had allowed him not to hit to humble him. That maybe God was trying to teach him a lesson in humility. He sat there and listened and then sadly answered, "Yes." We talked for a long time about pride, arrogance, and confidence. We talked about how God had blessed him with an exceptional talent but that it was all <u>from God.</u> We ended up praying together and he asked the lord to forgive him and he thanked Him for the talent God had given him. From that point on his hitting returned stronger than ever and I believe his eyes were more on the Lord for the blessing that He had given him.

In Daniel 4 there is a story about a King named Nebuchadnezzar who also had to learn some lessons in pride and humility. This King had a dream that he couldn't understand and he called for Daniel to come and interpret the dream to him. The dream went as follows: "There was a tree in the midst of the earth and its height was great. The tree grew large and strong, and its height reached to the sky and it was visible to the end of the whole earth. Its foliage was beautiful and its fruit abundant and in it was food for all. The beasts of the field found shade under it and the birds of the sky dwelt in its branches and all living creatures fed themselves from it.

Behold an angelic watcher a holy one, descended from heaven. He shouted out and spoke as follows," Chop down the tree and cut off its branches, strip off its foliage and scatter its fruit let the beasts flee from under it and the birds from its branches. Yet leave the stump with its roots in the ground, but with a band of iron and bronze around it in the new grass of the field; and let him be drenched with the dew of heaven, and let him share with the beasts in the grass of the earth. Let his mind be changed from that of a man, and let a beasts mind be given to him, and let seven periods of time pass over him. This sentence is by the decree of the angelic watchers and the decision is a command of the holy ones in order that the living may know that the Most High is ruler over the realm of mankind, and bestows it on whom He wishes, and sets over it the lowliest of men."

Daniel heard the Kings dream and said, "My Lord if only the dream applied to those who hate you and its interpretation to your adversaries! The tree that you saw which became large and grew strong who's height reached to the sky and visible to all the earth and whose foliage was beautiful and its fruit abundant and in which the beasts of the field dwelt and in whose branches the birds of the sky lodged – it is you, O King; for you have become great and grown strong and your majesty has become great and reached to the sky and your dominion to the end of the earth. And in that the King saw an angelic watcher a holy one descending from heaven and saying "Chop down the tree and destroy it; yet leave the stump with its roots in the ground but with a band of iron and bronze around it in the new grass of the field and let him be drenched with the dew of heaven and let him share with the beasts of the field until seven periods of time pass over him." "This is the interpretation, O King and this is the decree of the Most High which has come upon my Lord the King; that you be driven from mankind and your dwelling place be with the beasts of the field and you be given grass to eat like cattle and be drenched with the dew of heaven, and seven periods of time will pass over you, until you recognize that the Most High is ruler over the realm of mankind, and bestows it on whomever He wishes. And in that it was commanded to leave the stump with the roots of the tree, your Kingdom will be assured to you after you recognize that it is heaven that rules. Therefore O King may my advice be pleasing to you; break away now from your sins by doing righteousness, and from your iniquities by showing mercy to the poor, in case there may be a prolonging of your prosperity." Twelve months later the king was walking on the roof of the royal palace of Babylon. The King reflected and said "Is this not Babylon the great, which I myself have built as a royal residence by the might of my power and for the glory of my majesty?" While the word was in the Kings mouth a voice came from heaven saying, "King Nebuchadnezzar, to you it is declared: sovereignty has been removed from you."

From that moment on the King was driven away from mankind for seven years just like Daniels interpretation had said. At the end of the seven-year period the King said his reason had returned to him and he blessed the Most High and praised and honored Him. The Kings majesty and splendor were restored to him and he was reestablished in his sovereignty and surpassing greatness was added to him. The King also said something very poignant which was "Now I Nebuchadnezzar praise, exalt and honor the King of heaven, for all His works are true and His ways just, and He is able to humble those who walk in pride."

What a bitter sweet story this is, yet very vital to each of us. God does want to richly bless us in so many different ways. He desires to give us more than we could ever think or imagine. When he does though, and we think it's all about us, we're too much into ourselves and we need to be humbled. To forget that God is the giver of everything we have is a dangerous mind set to have. When we let pride come in and rule our hearts, God will use whatever means possible to get our attention back on him, and off of ourselves.

Proverbs 16:18 says this, "Pride goes before destruction and a haughty spirit before stumbling."

Everything in our lives, such as gifts, talents, health, family, financial blessings, is all from God and only Him. Everything that God gives us, we need to continually thank Him and give Him honor and praise. To realize that we wouldn't have anything if it weren't for Him and His goodness to us.

God Is Faithful

As parents we are constantly telling our kids, "Do the right thing," "Don't give into peer pressure," along with many other things. We tell them that if they do the right things they will be rewarded and blessed. Peer pressure is a very real thing for children, but also for adults as well. So many times we tell our kids what to do and what not to do yet we do not follow our own advice. As adults and parents we need to also as the saying goes, "Practice what we preach."

The story of Daniel in the lions' den is found in Daniel 6. This story goes along with not giving into pressure. To do what is right even if it means you're the only one doing it.

"Then the commissioners and satraps began trying to find a ground of accusation against Daniel in regard to government affairs; but they could find no ground of accusation or evidence of corruption, in as much as he was faithful, and no negligence or corruption was to be found in him. Then these men said "We shall not find any ground of accusation against this Daniel unless we find it against him with regard to the law of his God." Then these commissioners and satraps came by agreement to the king, and spoke to him as follows: "King Darius, live forever! All the commissioners of the kingdom, the prefects and the satraps, the high officials and the governors have consulted together that the King should establish a statute and enforce an injunction that anyone who makes a petition to any god or man besides you, O King, for thirty days, shall be cast into the lions' den. Now, O King, establish the injunction and sign the document so that it may not be changed, according to the law of Medes and Persians, which may not be revoked." Therefore King Darius signed the document, that is, the injunction. Now when Daniel knew that the document was signed, he entered his house (now in his roof chamber he has windows opened toward Jerusalem); and he continued kneeling on his knees three times a day, praying and giving thanks before his God, as he had been doing previously. Then these men came by agreement and found Daniel making petition and supplication before his God. Then they approached and spoke before the King about the Kings injunction, "Did you not sign an injunction that any man who makes a petition to any god or man besides you, O king, for thirty days is to be cast into the lions' den?" The king answered and said, "The statement is true, according to the law of the Medes and Persians which may not be revoked." Then they answered and spoke before the King. "Daniel, who is one of the exiles from Judah, pays no attention to you, O King, or to the injunction which you signed, but keeps making his petition three times a day." Then, as soon as the king heard this statement, he was deeply distressed and set his mind on delivering Daniel; even until sunset he kept exerting himself to rescue him. Then these men came by agreement to the King and said to the King, "Recognize, O king, that it is a law of the Medes and Persians that no injunction or statute which the King establishes may be changed." Then the King gave orders, and Daniel was brought in and cast into the lions' den. The King spoke and said to Daniel, "Your God whom you constantly serve will Himself deliver you." And a stone was brought and laid over the mouth of the den; and the king sealed it with his own signet ring and with the signet rings of his nobles, so that nothing might be changed in regard to Daniel. Then the King went off to his palace and spent the night fasting, and no entertainment was brought before him; and his sleep fled from him. Then the King arose with the dawn, at the break of day and went in haste to the lions' den. And when he had come near the den to Daniel, he cried out with a troubled voice. The King spoke and said to Daniel, "Daniel, servant of the living God, has your God, whom you constantly serve, been able to deliver you from the lions?" Then Daniel spoke to the King, O King, live-forever! My God has sent His angel and shut the lions' mouth, and they have not harmed me, in as much as I was found innocent before Him; and also toward you, O King, I have committed no crime." Then the King was very pleased and gave orders for Daniel to be taken up out of the den. So Daniel was taken up out of the den, and no injury whatever was found on him, because he had trusted his God."

So many times this story is just viewed that Daniel was saved from the lions that day and nothing else. Daniel was under "pressure" to not go against the statute but he chose God. He chose to fall to his knees with his windows open knowing he would be heard and seen. He didn't give in even though it could have cost him his life. He stood for what was right and he was blessed and his life was spared. He was face to face with the enemy that day. He had no way of escaping but God showed up and shut the enemies mouth for Daniel.

1 Peter 5:8, "Be of sober spirit, be on the alert. You adversary, the devil, prowls about like a roaring lion, seeking someone to devour."

Our enemy wants to devour us every day but our God is faithful and delivers us. When we live our lives faithfully to the Lord He is faithful to us in every situation.

2 Thessalonians 3:3, "But the Lord is faithful, and He will strengthen and protect you from the evil one."

No matter what the "lion" may come disguised as, it doesn't matter for us as Christians. Many "lions" come as financial problems, health issues, family stresses, etc. Our God though, through the story of Daniel, is showing us that it is He who shuts the lion's mouth every time for us.

1 John 4:5 says this, "You are from God, little children, and have overcome them; because greater is He who is in you than he who is in the world."

So, no matter how close the enemy seems to be, even face to face, know that God will shut the lion's mouth for you. He actually already shut its mouth when He redeemed us. Let's not forget that also.

Everlasting Love

When a couple first finds out that they are going to have a child they are instantly in awe. For the mom to be she knows there is a new life inside of her even though for a while she cannot feel any movement. The way technology is now we get to see that child in the mother's womb. Seeing that picture brings it all home for the parents to be. An instant bond of love is formed for those two expecting parents.

When the child is born it is so wonderful to actually hold, touch, and snuggle this little person you have loved for so long. Nothing can ever separate the love that parents have for their children. There may be some rough times through the years but that bond of love can never be broken.

God's love for us is even greater than that of an earthly love between a parent and child. God's word tells us in Jeremiah 1:5 this, "Before I formed you in the womb I knew you." That is something difficult for us to comprehend but it is the truth. To realize that even before we were in our moms tummy God knew each of us! Wow!

I John 3:1 says this, "See how great a love the Father has bestowed upon us, that we should be called children of God and such we are."

Now we know that God knew us before we were ever born, that we are His children and He loves us. Now just as earthly parents have an everlasting love for their children no matter what happens – what about God towards us?

Romans 8:37-39 reassures us of His love. "But in all these things we overwhelmingly conquer through Him who loved, for I am convinced that neither death, nor life, nor angels, nor principalities, nor things present, nor things to come, nor powers, nor height, nor depth, nor any other created thing, shall be able to separate us from the love of God, which is in Christ Jesus our Lord."

God is telling us that absolutely nothing could ever make Him not love us, nothing. He is so in love with each one of us that He gave His only begotten Son for us. We really cannot comprehend that kind of love here on earth. He knows every detail about us, about our lives and most of all He loves us and believes in us! His love for us is always the same. It does not vary based on our actions.

Jeremiah 31:3 says this, "I have loved you with an everlasting love."

You and I cannot truly understand how deeply God loves us. We tend to show love to others based on their actions or on our own moods. How selfish are we? Thankfully God does not love us how we love others. We are His children and He loves us so much more than we can imagine.

During your life here on this earth know that God in heaven, your Father loves you. Know that He is always aware of you and is constantly working on your behalf. Know that your thoughts, ideas, feelings, and your life matters to God. Know that even on those days when you feel no one cares or loves you, God your Father does and He always will.

Mission Possible

The movies called Mission Impossible really stretch the imagination. They make people think, "There's no way that could happen," yet they find themselves clued to the movie. Many people enjoy movies like that even though they know it's fictional. Somehow they get all caught up in the fantasy part of it all.

How about us though. Do we really believe nothing is impossible to us as Gods children?

Matthew 19:26 says this to us, "And looking upon them Jesus said to them, "With men this is impossible, but with God all things are possible."

We read this verse and can see the words but do we really truly believe the words? Do we really understand what God is telling us? Do we receive it as our own?

Think back to Moses in the Old Testament. Was the impossible made possible for him? He had many things happen that really blew people's minds, probably even his own. He witnessed the Red Sea being parted, manna being sent from heaven to feed the people, and he witnessed water flowing out of a rock so they could have something to drink! Talk about the impossible being made possible. That outweighs anything Hollywood could muster up! These are just three examples though. The Bible is filled with many examples of the impossible being made possible.

To many times though we tend to view these things as "the past." The thinking is, "God doesn't do things like that anymore." I tell you the truth that we ourselves have put God in a box and have limited Him. God is still the same God today that He was in the Bible. The same God who makes all things possible, and not just for them but for us as well. I myself know that nothing is impossible to us, nothing. My whole life God has continually shown me His faithfulness and power. We may not understand how God will work things out or even when but He will. When God opens or closes a door, they stay that way forever.

In God's word we read, over and over again, of God's faithfulness. We read some amazing and incredible stories. Stories that we just can't fathom. Seeing the Red Sea parted, receiving food from heaven, and even getting water from a rock seem so impossible to us but it happened.

The point is, EXPECT THE IMPOSSIBLE!! Whatever God has planned for you to accomplish in this world, He will equip you. He will make things happen that cannot be explained except it happened because of God.

1 Corinthians 1:25-27, "Because the foolishness of God is wiser than men; and the weakness of God is stronger than men. For ye see your calling, brethren, how that not many wise men after the flesh, not many mighty, not many noble are called; but God hath chosen the foolish things of the world to confound the wise and God hath chosen the weak things of the world to confound the things which are mighty."

God can do anything and He will. We just have to believe and have faith. God is looking for people who will believe and expect the impossible made possible.

Do not ever think, "Oh, that could never happen," or "That is just too big to believe God for." God tells us in Luke 1:45, "And blessed is she that believed that there would be a fulfillment of what had been spoken to her by the Lord."

Whatever God has shown you or spoken to you, believe it! It may seem totally illogical and impossible to you but nothing is impossible for God to do. If you want to see more of the impossible made possible, then I dare you to just believe and watch your mission made possible!

Go – Show and Tell

There will come a day for all parents when they must let their children go. Everything in life is about seasons and changes, including a child's life. They started out as helpless infants then slowly became more and more independent. Then the day arrives, that once helpless infant has graduated from High School and is preparing for college, and soon will leave the nest. The parents are left hoping and praying their child will have a great and successful life, and will remember all the goodness they have been taught. It's not a literal goodbye but a sendoff. That child will now have the responsibility of making their own way in life but will always have a home to come back to. The love and support will always be available to them.

Just as a child grows and moves on, so do we. Everything God does is for a season, and then it's time to move on to the next season. It's difficult at times to move on but it is also exciting. It's exciting to see where God is taking us and to see His plans for us revealed.

God created Praying Wives and Mothers, and it's the most beautiful ministry I have seen and been privileged to be a part of as I'm sure it is for you. Now though God wants to take you into another season. He wants to reveal more and more of Himself to you. He also wants you to take everything you have seen, learned, heard, and been healed from and share it with others.

Mark 16:15 tells all of us this, "Go into all the world and preach the gospel to all creation."

Many cannot literally go into the entire world, but all of us can minister in our own "backyard." We all have the same commission from Christ to spread the gospel and win souls for His Kingdom. We are to radiate Christ and His love to all mankind.

Luke 11:33, "No man when he hath lighted a candle, putteth it in a secret place, neither under a bushel, but on a candlestick, that they which come in may see the light."

We are to be the light of the world. To bring the light of Christ to the world. To show people that God loves them and has a plan for their lives. To tell them that they have been bought with a price, and there is forgiveness for all sins through Jesus' blood that was shed. To present hope to all men, showing them how much God loves and values them.

Throughout your coming diligently each week to this group God has taught you many things. He has been faithful, loving, and gracious towards you and He will continue. He is now asking you though, to be His light to all men. To take what God has shown and taught you, and bring the same good news to others. How will they know if they are not told? Some of the people that will be reached can only be reached through you. God has put people in your life for many reasons and for some it's for spreading the good news that can only be shared to them by you.

Perhaps God has or will call you to be a group leader of Praying Wives and Mothers to minister to others. Perhaps He hasn't called you for that, but He has called you to go out and tell of Him and His goodness. I do not know the plan God has for each for you but I do know, whatever it may be, it is wonderful. He though, requires of us to spread His message to everyone we can. To show the power of God and His transforming love that is available to everyone.

As you end this season in your life may you also be filled with excitement for the next season. May you realize how wonderful He is for bringing Praying Wives and Mothers into your life, and for all He has taught and given unto you. May God richly bless you and your faithfulness to Him. May His face always shine upon you as His child and servant.

Praying Wives and Mothers
MINISTRIES

Praying Wives and Mothers Ministries is a place where women can safely learn their value and the love the Father has for them. A place where women can globally connect through the power of prayer, and be the women God has designed them to be.

www.prayingwivesandmothersministries.org

gina@prayingwivesandmothersministries.org

Made in the USA
Monee, IL
18 March 2020